The Truth Seeker's Handbook

Also by Roger Brown:
Insights
Heading Out
Encounters
33 Years of Dreams

Note that the first two sections of the Truth Seeker's Handbook have been published as their own books:

Themes of my Life
Reminders From Life, for Life

# The Truth Seeker's Handbook

A spiritual guide for life on Earth

# Roger Golden Brown

Golden Galaxy Publications

Published by Golden Galaxy Publications
Copyright 2015 Roger Golden Brown
ISBN: 978-0-9743513-2-2

You are free to copy and redistribute the material under the following terms:

Attribution - You must give appropriate credit and indicate if changes were made. You may do so in any reasonable manner, but not in any way that suggests that I endorse you or your use.

ShareAlike - If you change the material in any way, you must distribute your contributions under this same license.

No additional restrictions - You may not apply legal terms that legally restrict others from doing anything this license permits.

Please contact me if you have any questions.

I can be contacted at the following e-mail address:
wordsmith@goldengalaxies.net

Visit my personal website:
https://goldengalaxies.net/

And check out my world affairs oriented website:
https://goldengalaxies.net/Quasar/

This book is available for sale at:
http://books2read.com/truthseekershandbook

See all of my books at my Author Page:
http://books2read.com/rogergoldenbrown

Only the road and the dawn, the sun, the wind, and the rain,
And the watch fire under stars, and sleep, and the road again.

John Masefield

# Preface

I was born to a British mother and a father whose family tree goes back to the 1500's in America. I grew up in the woods, north of Seattle. I was raised a Quaker. My father was an inspiration in every sense, a spiritually oriented man of high integrity. Also my entrance onto the Earth scene was timed to be someone born to be at the heart of the hippie movement and to contribute to helping the world change for the better. I was also born an Aquarian. And I embrace that as I identify physically as a world citizen and spiritually as a player in the greater scheme of things.

I have lived in many places, done quite a potpourri of work, and have known many unique individuals. Amidst the variety that spiced my life an integral part of a significant period of time was writing in journals. This started on San Jaun Island in Washington State in 1975. Through good times and hard times I wrote almost daily for over 20 years, recording observations, thoughts, feelings, dreams (both the nighttime and the aspirational varieties), and experiences; both physical experiences and some more etheric experiences.

Life is a trip. Amidst the uncertainties, during this journey, I have tried to at least be aware of what is going on around me and what is going on within me. Using entries from my journals and elaborating on them, I have put together writings that make up this book.

It is in 4 parts:

**Themes** consists of a number of themes that developed naturally from my journals writings that go to some of the core issues of life.

**Reminders** is a collection of short entries that are perhaps philosophy if they are deep enough to qualify as that; references for daily living.

**Earth in Peril** is a look at the inner relationship that we have with the planet and the reasons why we do harm to our home.

**True Stories** is just that; a few tales from my life and of some of the serendipity I have experienced and the interesting people I have encountered.

The reader may notice that some passages found in Themes are repeated in or as Reminders. I decided to let that be because I felt that it was important to keep Reminders intact. I have found that for myself Reminders functions well as a bedside book to be browsed on a regular basis, offering nudges towards action or attitude.

So… fellow sojourner. Welcome.

## Contents

Themes ................................................................. 1

Reminders ........................................................... 90

Earth in Peril .................................................... 129

True Stories ...................................................... 172

About the Author ............................................. 230

Other Books by Roger Brown ......................... 231

# Themes

Throughout the 97 volumes of journals that I have filled there are various thoughts and observations and epiphanies that I have had that seem to recur. They arise in many different contexts. And they take many different forms but over time and with ongoing reflection, they seem to have coalesced into themes that I have found to be cogent and helpful.

## Themes Contents

Honesty...................................................2
Hoax......................................................11
God and Participation......................17
Evil........................................................22
Committee Members........................31
Consumer Consciousness................37
True Efficiency..................................42
Tourist in Life Concept...................48
True Love............................................53
Life Between and Behind the Lines...............59
Karma and Grace..............................64
The Golden Rule Dilemma.............71
Imagination........................................76
Sensing, Feeling, Thinking..............83

# Honesty

This theme is just a primer on some basic principles of honesty and the virtues - no, on the functional necessity of honesty. I believe it underlies virtually every learning tool on the road to heaven. The ability to learn from mistakes, the act of forgiving, any community or team or friendship efforts, or a personal confidence that will endure - all rely on honesty or they will inevitably go awry.

- - -

As the world is shrinking faster and faster I feel a sense of optimism. Although I am discouraged often with how people behave, I see ultimately how the growing closer will lead to union.

I call it the tower of lies. When you lie, you create a structure that needs supporting by more lies. Who hasn't discovered the difficulty of not telling the truth and had to keep covering their tracks with more fabrications. For this structure to sustain itself it must have a place to hide the truth. One method is to blame someone else or discredit someone or some information, so that a conflicting story can't damage the preferred story. The problem with this is that it requires dark areas, secrets, and enemies. Enemies who we can say want to distort the truth for their own wicked agenda.

But as information and communication systems become more and more available, dark areas cease to exist. And with the ease of travel and even the exposure of television, we have learned that even in the countries led by "bad guys" the people are not vermin. They cry for their families and children too. It's slow; denial is a powerful technique to ease the pain. But slowly the truth will out. The tower of lies gets more and more rickety as it gets higher and higher. The stresses increase and eventually it collapses.

- - -

You can only tell so many lies before it's clear that it doesn't make any sense. When you're dishonest you're forever trying to figure out what is going on. If everyone was straight and honest we would know what was going on. Be honest, be real, know where you stand. Ultimately, honesty is the path of least friction. The truth always dovetails.

- - -

Yes, we must be honest. With my tower of lies analogy, I was mostly addressing the societal realm. But honesty is equally, or perhaps more important in our personal relationships. Don't dissemble and smooth things over. That smoothness is an illusion. Tell it like it is. We may lose friends but we'll surely gain others and bring a higher grade into our lives. If the truth drives someone or something away from you, then what did you have anyway? Imagine a world where everyone was honest. We'd all know what each other wanted. It would be so much easier to help and to solve problems.

What's more, honesty must be more than just not lying when directly confronted with something. It must be sharing with the intention of helping each other understand so all involved can be clear.

- - -

And if we truly hope to interact with others with honesty and integrity we must first be fully honest with ourselves. Being really truthful and open is how one finds oneself into the beauty that unfolds. Just like growing a flower or a fruit, love is the agreement with natural law. If you use poisons or try and manipulate the system, you spend energy forever trying to manipulate it back into order. Loving and open honesty are the keywords of spiritual ecology.

- - -

In life it is often beneficial to seek balance. Regarding honesty, however, it's not necessary to seek the balance. Truth and honesty are pure in and of themselves, not needing a balance. It's the honesty of our actions that gives the balance.

- - -

From the book, Illusions: "Your conscience is the measure of the honesty of your selfishness." Now what the heck does that mean, you might ask.

It's so simple, really. Unity is the source of pleasure. When we are "together", we are unified within ourselves, and can easily fit without. Like if you are "centered", "together", "home", you can see clearly out. To not be honest, to not act in confidence, to fear and consequently to try and manipulate outcomes, you accede to satisfy the needs of the armor, the responses to protect us from the assaults on ourselves from past experiences. Then it's like being a bent piece and trying to fit in the puzzle. Honesty and selfish confidence are the candles for the yet to be illuminated new frontiers outside the armor.

If we can shuck the guilt that says it's not ok to be selfish, if we are honest about our selfishness, our power increases; our intent becomes more unified, and we become more effective. Paradoxically, our conscience would be clearer to give "unselfishly."

- - -

A short story about honesty:

During a time when I was building massage tables for a living, I learned a valuable lesson with the aid of a good friend. I had just finished a table and noticed a teensy hole in the vinyl. It really bummed me out. I didn't know if I should let it go or tell the clients who were coming over to buy it.

My friend Ken called and I mentioned it to him. He said that we often try and guess people's reactions and don't give them credit and usually imagine worse scenarios than what would probably happen if we were open. The situation, the problem/possibility, was that two women were coming over together for two tables and since I only had two tables done, one would have to make a compromise.

Well, I told them and it was a bit of a dilemma but the humor was good and I offered possibilities; to redo it or give a reduction, maybe 5, 10 or 15 dollars. I left the room and left them alone and when I came back they had decided who would take it for $15 off. It was good vibes all around.

- - -

Delight in truth at all costs.

We really must accept everything we experience. Simply say, yes, this is happening to me. We tend to avoid and repress and choose against less pleasant feelings. What a rip-off! They offer powerful information as to what is going on; information as to the reason why we don't at the moment have pleasant feelings. The desirable feelings validate flow and rightness. The unpleasant ones are the ones needing the most attention.

- - -

This journal entry is a great example of this:

Tonight my ear hurts. I'm asking myself about it. I was tempted to say, "what is wrong with my ear?" How awful. If one must think in terms of "wrong" a more accurate and helpful approach would be to ask, "what's wrong with my truth?" More accurately, "what's lacking in my truth that my ear is alerting me to?"

It's your basic: If you do it right, it's gone. If you do it wrong, it's still there.

What part of myself, related to this ear pain, (pain = alert) is being held out of harmonious flow in denial? Which is to say out of consciousness.

You have to bring things into consciousness out of their lairs into the light.... then let them, with awareness, slip away out of consciousness.

- - -

I conclude the honesty theme with a sub-theme:

## Reality is Synonymous With Power

On deeper levels honesty must also include a dedication to validating all that we think and all that we feel and all that our senses perceive. This fits in with what I said about "information" and the tower of lies. All information is good information. Don't blame the messenger. We must validate all that we perceive. Anything less leads us on a wild goose chase. And leaves us open to the mass hypnosis of the planetary paradigms; not to mention the powerful norms of every little clique a person may associate with. A true measure of friendship would be the amount of allowance and even encouragement one offers another to explore a reality that is engendered by their own thoughts, feelings, and senses.

- - -

Some of my favorite lines from the Doors are in this final stanza of the song, Strange Days.

- - -

> Strange days have found us
> And through their strange hours
> We linger alone
> Bodies confused
> Memories misused
> As we run from the day
> To a strange night of stone

- - -

Bodies confused, memories misused. Think about what is being said here. When any information is distorted to fit into some kind of preconceived idea, it leaves the body confused. If someone feels sexual desire but their religion tells them that such feelings are bad, it will certainly confuse the body. If pain or discomfort is masked by drugs the body is cheated out of the information it needs and the natural biofeedback it needs to take the best path to healing itself and to learn for future similar situations.

If someone feels greedy, but because of some spiritual belief that tells them that they should feel all-giving and one with all, they might suppress it or camouflage it and they will have installed a memory that is false. If someone feels abused by a friend, but feels that the friendship means too much to be compromised by bad feelings, they may convince themselves that it wasn't really like that in an attempt to soften the conflict. And, of course, there are the basics like denial and justification, pretending something really didn't happen or inventing reasons for feelings or acts so they don't go against a self image, or whatever style is perceived to be one's own.

When you are running your life and trying to modify your behavior, no matter how good your intentions are, if you are drawing on memories that aren't real; that aren't honest, then you are traveling a muddy road. It's the old how can you get to where you'd like to go if you don't know where you are. You are running "from the day to a strange night of stone." Where there could be light and self-improvement, although possibly challenging, there is darkness and rigidity.

Yes, reality is synonymous with power.

- - -

Endeavor to not cheat yourself out of reality, out of your own reality as you mingle with and communicate with people who do not want to know the true nature of things; who would happily gloss over the awkward. It's ok to share but stick up for your reality, at least remain aware of it.

It might seem that this might leave you lonely or separate from those whose small talk avoids the complexities (and with it, the beauty) of the human condition. But this is not true. Paradoxically you may find that relationships will become easier when you're not trying to accommodate others people's worlds by altering you own perception of reality. Just say, "here I am, here's what I see, you can take it or leave it." You have nothing to hide because you've got nothing to alter. You are at your best.

# Themes

---

This from my journals:

A couple of nights ago I was thinking about Gina and phantasizing being close to her and thinking how my feelings really would want her, even though I know any phantasy of continued togetherness is pretty inappropriate. Not the phantasy (nothing inappropriate there), but the reality of acting on it, I mean. Which is the point. I recognized that as my will and wisdom become more capable I can allow myself to recognize real feelings, because I don't feel afraid that I'll act inappropriately on those feelings. I can allow myself to feel lust for women who are too young or too anything to actually get involved with. I can allow myself to feel anger towards someone without having to "do" anything about it. And on and on. And what that does is allow me to better let these feelings flow, to observe them freer of bodies confused and memories misused. They can play themselves out undistorted.

---

When intense feelings would compel a person into destructive or radically challenging acts, I think those feelings are suppressed to avoid that. Keeping as much as possible of the current reality of your life validated helps you become clearer and gives more room for past baggage to come back which can now be handled and released, in the light of reality.

---

As one becomes freer and clearer, the honest pictures, unfiltered and undiluted can come out and be learned from. Bodies will not be confused and memories will not be misused. I can entertain phantasies and I can allow all thoughts and urges conscious awareness because I have less and less guilt about the implications of that. I have more and more faith in my ability to behave lovingly with consideration for higher spiritual concerns and golden sharings and allowings. And more and more ability to feel it, let it go, and release as I go.

Guilt is a big reason why people get muddled. It's why people need law. They don't trust themselves to behave. Guilt is like that internal law. "I can't (allow myself to) feel that. If I feel that without guilt, if I let myself have, or worse, enjoy that feeling, just think of what horrible things I might do."

But it's a short term solution. And suppressed, those feelings will eventually explode and manifest in confusion, distress, or disharmonious behavior.

- - -

Let me repeat:
How can you get to where you'd like to go if you don't know where you are?
The truth always dovetails.
Delight in truth at all costs.
Reality is synonymous with power.

# Hoax

It was near the winter solstice when I went to see Brother Sun, Sister Moon, the beautiful Zeffirelli film. I was deeply moved. Saint Francis had given up the life of a wealthy family to help others and spend his life in service. Clare, the woman he loved, stayed behind continuing her life as it was.

Later in the film after she has had an epiphany, she finds him and says to him, "I don't want to be loved anymore, I want to love. I don't want to be understood any longer, I want to understand."

I left the theater feeling a determination to open to loving; to really know I have something to give.

- - -

The desire to really prioritize giving and loving really came home to me two months later. It had been getting a bit springish in Santa Cruz where I was living at the time, and one special day it was in the 80's with a luscious wind blowing off the mountains.

A part of me woke up. I would call it an epiphany except that it was too native and too much of the body, too much embodied in me to call it anything like a realization. It was a knowing.

I went out into the day and felt such a rush of love; physical as well as emotional. I could feel my hands tenderly aching to give. My breathing was from the depth of my gut. I spent the day, first at home, then outside in the country and finally in town among my fellow gods, rushing, drunk on longing to love.

Yes! It's all a big fake.
Perpetrated by those of low confidence,
by those who feel little.
The hoax that we need to be loved.

- - -

It's easy to get stuck in the fear to admit that we are Great enough and Full enough to love so beautifully; that our real need is to give love. To run it. To flood it out onto fellow humans.

We've got to believe that we've got something to give.

What is it to be human? Whether it is from the oxygen we breath in or the energy showered upon us by the cosmos, or simply the stuff of life bestowed on us at birth, energy is life. Energy comes in and energy goes out. We are, in effect, a transmitting station. The thing is to decide; to feel if it goes out in pain or if it goes out in art, if it goes out in hate and fear or if it goes out in loving.

As Wilhelm Reich said regarding this, "It is really the only question. And the one that is never asked." Going into Wilhelm Reich now would be out of the scope of this writing but a main theme of his deserves some mention. And that is that when you draw your energy in, in fear, you contract. When you send energy out, in love, you expand. And this expansion is the essence of what enriches life giving us health on all levels.

- - -

There have been times when I have caught myself caught up in the flux of emotions relative to daily life and I have felt myself wanting to be loved; wanting love to come to me. Not feeling enough within. It's not an altogether good feeling. There is a human richness to it but it also feels weak.

I would suggest that at such times simply try and live what grace you can here and now and work work work on keeping the energy and love energy flowing out and not give into the hoax of trying to draw things towards yourself.

I admit to neediness. But there have also been times when I felt that I was enough within to give, not needing anything coming back. And it is a clean feeling of power. At such times one thing I have noticed that accompanies this feeling is that I feel no sense of being a victim and no sense of self pity for what I don't have.

But let me be clear that in recognizing the hoax and that the highest energy is to be giving love, there is no conflict between that and the receiving of love. In fact, the expansion and openness when one is giving allows love in more easily than when we feel needy and contract. There is also a bit of a paradox here. And that is that when you can fully receive, free of any implications; when you can just simply take it, then you know, really know, what giving is and that it's worth it. Recognize and accept the gifts you are given as part of the whole. Then complete the circle. Circulate that energy back out into the world.

- - -

The following is an excerpt from my journals; a bit of struggling with believing in the hoax but feeling stuck:

> What is recognizing my power and purity; my good intentions? And what is selfish? And how much selfishness am I entitled to? Can't I do (be) both?
>
> Maybe it's just that if I'm looking for physical ends, I need to employ physical means. Without

diluting or cheapening my spiritual quest, I need to be equal in my validation of my physical quest. Be of unified heart; of unified mind; of unified application of self. It's all one package. I'm all one package.

That also means taking a physically realistic look at where I want to be, where I am, and how to play the game. "Realistic" meaning how it works now; whether it is a social or a personal paradigm.

I'm reminded of one of the basics that recurred often in the Edgar Cayce readings. "Bring your ideals into your personality." Maybe that is the bridge between spiritual ideals and physical "needs."

- - -

The iron stove story; how the hoax works socially as well:

My friend and roommate Michael wanted to build a hot tub and use a wood stove to heat it. I had noticed an old iron stove in an alley while bike riding and a couple of days later I went by and asked the owners about it. They gave it to me. It was in good shape and all the parts were there.

When I went, it was just to get it for Michael, but when I got it and checked it out I felt greedy and wanted to keep it or sell it or something.

But I felt kind of bad about that and when I brought it home, I told Michael that I felt a little greedy about it and it might fit in my sauna (which currently had a stove in it). He didn't seem to understand what I was trying to say and after we looked at it, said "thanks", mistakenly accepting it as a gift.

Any greed I had had disappeared in the next couple of minutes. It just felt good to let it go and pass it on and have it used. I felt clearly and cleanly how that facilitates a tight knit functional economy. A tight knit functional energy output, production, use, time, effective economy.

Capitalist communism.

Objects aren't owned collectively and shared by legislated order. It's just that if we function as a team, there isn't surplus clogging everything up. Privately "owned" objects, (as much as one can own anything) are given up like feeding the open player in basketball.

- - -

I can't get out of the Hoax theme without at least a passing mention of sex.

Hungry for sex, once, I realized very clearly that satisfied doesn't mean getting sex; it means getting fulfillment or completion in some way; feeling unity and loved and loving.

When these needs aren't met the desire for sex serves as a means to satisfaction. Not that sex isn't a part of that satisfying. Just that it will never be the solution. And I think when one is unsatisfied and feels that charge, it is so primal and therefore immediate that it takes wisdom to keep attention on our real needs.

- - -

While it's natural to want and to hope to get strokes for accomplishments and to receive love and attention, instead realize that "results" such as successes and failures are all part of the whole. And the more you participate and the more that you are an active agent for the greater good, then what you might have seen before as a success, you now recognize as a part of the flow and part of the bigger picture.

Perhaps what might have been seen as a highlight, is now seen as an integral part of the light.

- - -

Finally, I would say that believing in the hoax doesn't mean that acting as a channel of giving love is as simple as reminding oneself. The paradigm of getting and accumulating and requiring is pervasive. Just try and keep your eye on the prize: love as an organic all-inclusive comprehensive way of life.

Acts are best done in the spirit of giving, not as a duty but as our birthright and because it is the essence of health on all levels; done in the spirit of unity. "Success" is not an isolated over and done with tangible thing, but rather the smooth functioning of the whole.

# God and Participation

Yesterday was cool! I rounded a corner, took a breath, saw a yellow rose (generally my favorite color by smell), and a butterfly fluttered by. I noticed the trees didn't just blow in the breeze, but shimmered. Clouds weren't just in the sky. They hung there, gently morphing.

It was like Rod Serling's Twilight Zone. The surroundings are the same but something has changed. You've entered the Twilight Zone.

In my case I felt I'd entered the God Zone.

Visually, things had nice crisp edges. And like a good nostalgia trigger, smells had a crisp edged quality to them.

But, paradoxically, they somehow, kinda, sorta, hung together as one. (Maybe as "One." Big "O".)

I looked up. It just seemed I should look up. So I looked up in the sky and I saw God (That's where God is, up in the sky, right.) I think it's just because when you look up you look out and when you look down you look in. Though I have noticed that if you look far enough out you're looking in again…. but that's a different story…. Wait a minute. Maybe that isn't a different story. That is this story.

But it wasn't really only in the sky I saw God. (Yeah. Big "G" God.) It's like we're in the Milky Way but you don't see it just glancing to the right or left. No, you look far out you see it in the sky and we're hangin' on the edge.

It came to me. So clearly. Simple really; clear crisp edged thoughts and ideas that, however, weren't limited. Maybe an epiphany is something that seems like it should be, used to be, and maybe "normally" is weird… but now not. It's fantastic, but it's right where and when it's supposed to be. "However humble, there's no place like…."

God.

At that moment the idea of God was not difficult or mystifying or mystified. It wasn't only for the religious or the devout. God is…. well, …. I could see at that moment that God cannot be defined in terms of anything in time, space, or matter as a definitive being. I saw that as one gets more in tune, thinking and acting more in unity, one gets closer to God and the closer to God one gets the more the separation begins to break down and God and the beholder approach unity. There would be no ego separation that could or would (even if it was desired, which I'm sure at this point, it wouldn't be) distinguish God as a specific form or being. The relationship is dynamic. I used the words "closer to God." It's more like more integrated.

Edgar Cayce, the great psychic, in one of his psychic readings, described God as being within oneself first, then manifest outside, as all of our's God. The Universal Mind.

Certainly we've all heard many variations of "we are all one" and "God is everywhere in everything."

Perhaps the idea of a single entity "God" is not incompatible with this. Perhaps, we do all, indeed, as the truest form of God, combine to form a Universal Mind or spirit. But here on earth there are very few of us humble souls who are free enough to reach a high level of unity that supports a fully integrated Universal Mind, especially when we are wrapped up in our daily life concerns and agendas. But, the Universal Mind is made up of all consciousness, not just human and earthly, and in spite of the relative insufficiencies of most of us, it has incredible integrity and power. So, to us, it would appear to be a unit, a single being, an intelligence, a mind, or a spirit that is all knowing and holy. It is not apart from us; it is simply a part of us; the purest center and concentration, seen from the outlands.

- - -

And how do our actions, the acts we carry out, fit into the idea of unity. It's like a player in a team sport who feels no sense of disappointment at not having had a chance to make a particular play when a teammate makes it and succeeds for the whole. The feeling is pure support for the action which successfully benefits the whole.

And as you act for the team you realize that expectations or demands for personal recognition or rewards put on life or the universe must be transcended. Instead of thinking in terms of personal success or personal rewards you now simply recognize accomplishments as a facet of the "everything" that you participate in.

You have just moved a little bit closer to the center of God. Or, if you prefer, you have moved a little closer to complete union with "One." I struggle with words here to not put anyone off. You get the picture. Find your own words. Or perhaps, if you can feel it without words, you're even closer.

- - -

Influenced by reading the book Right Use of Will talking of always loving yourself unconditionally, I told myself over and over to do so and looked around at myself and others and tried to see everyone as gods, kind of roaming around on earth. Since then it has been very powerful for me to see my fellow sojourners as little gods roaming around, interacting, emoting, sharing. I believe this is a really powerful way to look out at the world; maybe because it is really true. We are all divine and equal as spirits. Here is me in a journal entry seeing people this way:

> In the co-op this evening I was in a really serene state, looking at people in various ways attractive to me and often really looking and feeling, moving on and actually laughing at.... I'm not sure.... laughing at their beauty?, in my freedom?, the gentle way they carry on?, seeing people as little gods, kinda milling around, weaving individual acts into what it is on this planet.

What I find interesting is how positive the whole picture was that I described. Beauty. Freedom. These qualities are natural to us all and even when we find things to be critical about, it is helpful to remember that we are indeed little gods and all contributors to the universal mind and a greater God.

- - -

And there is a personal element related to the participation aspect of getting closer to the center of God. Reflecting on the paradox of as you get to know yourself better, you are more able to sense yourself as a part of the whole and in unity with all, I saw clearly how that makes sense. You might think that putting energy into getting to know yourself would make you more into separateness but actually what is happening is that lots of energy and behavior and responses that aren't yours are removed and that leaves you clearer in your role as a dynamic vital participant. Which is different than a togetherness with little or no personal soul searching because when programmed responses dominate your behavior you are in one respect more together with others – intertwined - but it is your mucky psychology and dominating, need to control side that is interacting. This explains also the perspective of the 1st chakra family tribe nation love that moves people so deeply; the patriotic attachments that make people feel so much attraction to one person while having animosity for others who are different. It's a bad dance. Free of that programming, the chemistry gets better and better.

So it is important that we must be a participant at all levels. Be aware of ourselves as gods in the greater scheme of things and be aware of ourselves as imperfect individuals increasing our self awareness in order to function as smoothly as possible.

# Evil

The word evil is such a hot word and a real button for many people. It sounds so dark and it is so often used as an absolute. In conversations it can really set people off. Visions of Hitler or slavery arise. Some don't believe in it at all and others believe we are all evil, while still others believe they are not and certain other people or groups are inherently evil. But I maintain that evil is not one fixed state of being that is reserved for the most dastardly people. It is an element of life as a human. And it exists in many different amounts in each person. Also it is not an absolute within any one person. A person may act in an evil way under one set of circumstances and not under another. Or under one set of circumstances at one time, and then not under similar circumstances at another time. What's more, I think one needs to be clear that evil is not the opposite of good.

It may be easier to just look at the world as good guys and bad guys but that insults the potential we all have to deal with the complexities of the human condition.

- - -

So, what is evil by my reckoning?

I read a friend of mine a dream I'd had about being obstructed by evil souls and she took exception to the concept of evil. I said I viewed it simply as the other end of the spectrum from harmony. And that now I do believe in evil beings; simply as those whose pain and solitude is so intense that they will do anything to anyone to keep from having their hoax exposed; to keep from having to face themselves.

But I believe I should modify the above. That is too absolute. There is no pure evil. It's all relative. Intensely evil might dominate and abuse huge amounts of people or mildly evil might just be willing to ruin your day to mask some pain. And within any being evil or lack of it is not absolute. It depends on the moment. Life is after all a series of choices.

My friend answered me in saying, "but it wasn't intentional and if it's not intentional, it's not evil."

I said certainly it is intentional. It is unconscious, but intentional, none the less. The choices she and I make every day with awareness are buried many layers down for many people. And within the limits of our enlightenment we too probably take actions to protect ourselves from exposing our weaknesses; that with which we are out of harmony. And, it is true, in every part of the spectrum, people seek to control others for their own validation. I guess that's really a challenge to try and not coerce any one in order to support our insufficiencies. And to be aware when we do.

- - -

In another dream I was trying to define evil. It was very specifically explained. Here are the words I used in my dream. "Whenever, whoever doesn't allow anyone, anytime to do what they want." But I was uncertain about the "to do what they want" part and tossed around alternatives like "freedom." Struggling with the end went on a long time.

When I wrote it down it seemed like me telling me to allow everyone their own path. Which is also me telling me to allow me my own path. It's circular.

- - -

Also I would go so far as to say that there are no evil thoughts. Only evil acts. On this stage on earth we are here as souls to learn in the physical plane, where we choose to manifest impulses physically. And grow and improve ourselves depending on our choices.

In the original Star Trek TV series there was an episode called A Taste Of Armageddon in which, when Kirk destroys the machines that sanitized their war, the people were horrified of the possibility of facing the true ugliness of war.

Kirk gave the following soliloquy:

"War is instinctive. But the instinct can be fought. We're human beings with the blood of a million savage years on our hands! But we can stop it. We can admit that we're killers ... but we're not going to kill today. That's all it takes! Knowing that we're not going to kill ….. today!"

So the thoughts are there. Do we act on them and create disharmony? Or do we rise above the impulse for the betterment of ourselves and all around us?

- - -

Although I said that there are no evil thoughts, only evil acts, there is inner turmoil generated by lack of willingness to take life and its complexities on without imposing your will on others. Hate is one such manifestation of this turmoil. And although hate is not in and of itself evil, if not dealt with within, it can often lead to evil manifest.

I once had a clear realization about reasons to hate.

It came clear to me that people don't have reasons to hate. They just want to hate and find reasons to justify their hate. If the plantation owner didn't have the niggers to hate it would be his wife or neighbor. If the redneck didn't have the hippie to hate it would be his boss or the guy who sold him some shoddy merchandise. If the hippie didn't have Nixon to hate it would be the neighbor's dog or the weather.

And it came to me that we can look at levels of justifying hate as a barometer of our growth and enlightenment. And we can (and do, on some level of awareness) use that barometer to constantly be letting go of baggage (becoming en-lighten-ed), continually changing the filter that finds "good" reasons to justify hating whatever it is that you hate.

This helps cleansing the self of justification for acts of evil and, of course, helps us move closer to the center of God.

- - -

It seems clear, looking at the spectrum of individuals this way, that truly no acts of aggression or "evil" are personal. They are simply acting and reacting in fear response with emotional baggage.

And there is a connection between how people hurt other people and/or hurt the environment. Everybody does what they think gives them power.

Here's an example of that. The other day, my brother was telling me how some loggers, for a demonstration against the environmentalists, drove their trucks around and how crude it seemed to him.

It struck me how perfect it was. That's where they get their power. A person with more faith in the ether might stand quietly with a candle, because that's where they get their power. Or at least, in both cases, where these people think or believe they get their power. I realized that essentially that's what we all do, to some extent all the time; everything we do, every act. We do what we think gives us our power, brings us our power, leads us to our power.

That doesn't seem to explain how often we, as humans, seem to waste our power or choose paths of denial and avoidance of positive responsible behavior.

That's the trap. We might waste time or act out physically in ways that fall short of our ideals or seem to exhibit a real lack of introspection, but that is us choosing the shortsightedness of the avoidance of the pain or discomfort of acts that challenge our status quo. Avoiding a challenge and the struggle to overcome the way we are can seem to give us more power than the outcome of the struggle would ultimately give us.

And perhaps the challenge in all growth and spiritual unfoldment is to recognize as a learner, or show, as a teacher, that the result of taking on challenges and breaking through will lead to a kind of harmony and flow and trust and faith that really does increase our power.

- - -

I want to wrap up this section on the evil theme with a story of an example of evil manifested by good people with all good intentions. At the time the incident struck me as being in essence very similar to the concept of fascism, assuming the right to control others, believing themselves to be superior or authorized.

I looked up fascism and came up with this definition:

> Any movement, ideology, or attitude that favors dictatorial government, centralized control of private enterprise, repression of all opposition, and favors extreme nationalism. The most notable

characteristic of a fascist country is the separation and persecution or denial of equality to a specific segment of the population based upon superficial qualities or belief systems. Simply stated, a fascist government always has one class of citizens that is considered superior (good) to another (bad) based upon race, creed or origin.

Now, although this definition defines fascism in terms of a government, the concept applies also to individuals whose actions dominate others. The story:

Some years ago I built and sold massage tables. One day a woman I knew, Annie, came over with a massage therapist friend Jenni, to look at my tables to maybe buy one. The following is the excerpt from my journals:

> Somehow the subject of doing massage without a license came up with me maintaining that why should anyone need the government's approval to choose to pay anyone for a massage. It was a major button for them. Jenni said it's a good thing that massage therapists must be licensed. She had her reasons. Shoddy arguments. They both said, as the conversation developed, that it was very complicated. God, how simple can it be. Choice. Freedom. No victims. She said it was simpler in a state where a license is required; she's not called up for sex. It's like an ad in Penthouse I once saw, about censorship. Yes, now your life is a lot simpler and a little less free.
>
> I explained the Profound Simplicity of choice and she couldn't get past the fear. She was worried

that somebody messing with your energy who doesn't know what they are doing could be really bad.

Regarding my views, Annie said they were so idealistic. Yeah, so what?! If not us, who? If not now, when? Haven't we slaughtered and dominated enough for enough centuries, millennia because adults have concluded that ideals are teenage stuff and not attainable in, they say, the "real world."

I'll sit at your round table, Arthur.

It was just amazing hearing Jenni defend a small group of people's right to legislate their ethics. She defended it saying it wasn't the government; it was a group of massage therapists.

God, every fascist state will tell you their experts know best and should decide the standards. Who cares who they are? Who decides who gets to decide?! There are no victims. It really is that simple.

It was weird too. I felt very harsh talking my talk. In the face of their resistance, my concepts were an affront on crystallized concluded battle lines of right and wrong. In a healthy sane world it would have been reversed. Her imposition on my freedom would have seemed very harsh indeed.

The paradigm and hypnosis of fear. It really is the essence of evil. Fear that a world of choice by individuals taking responsibility for themselves is too dangerous and we need control by authorities to protect us.

And how freely and without the simplest critical thinking it is assumed that a particular group of people have a bead on what is right and best and safest and, most importantly, necessary.

It hurts to meet intelligent, caring, sensitive people who just can't see the simplest of freedoms. Choice, victimless crimes.

One more thing. If someone sees the logic and truth in freedom of choice but still thinks we need controls and limits, I ask again:

Can it really be that we live in a world where doing what is right, won't work? It's all so clouded in complex scenarios of tragedy, but it really is so simple.

It comes back to my definition of evil. That battle line of right and wrong is determined by fear. When the light (of reason, of truth) begins to compel a person to face their denials but threatens to compromise what they perceive as their security, it is at this point, if the light does not prevail, where they begin to need to control their environment, abusing and dominating others (beings, creatures, nature) to protect their lie and avoid having to deal with complexities and their personal inner struggle.

- - -

And finally, something else that ties in with the idea of people controlling others. And that is that one of the biggest problems in the world is that people don't believe that doing what is right will work, when in fact it is the only thing that will work. In this case a dominant social paradigm is reinforced by those who lack vision and/or faith.

You hear it in religion, you hear it in politics, you hear it socially. "Yeah, that would be the ideal thing to do but it won't work in the real world." People are forever accepting destructiveness, inequality, and compromises to integrity because they don't believe that doing the right thing will work. And the paradigm is reinforced and feeds itself and makes the right thing ever more incompatible with *their* real world.

As a friend of mine once said, "anything that isn't value oriented, is doomed to failure."

## Committee Members

I had an experience once with a person with whom I had been very close and who had expressed her interest and excitement in our friendship, then for no reason apparent to me, decided that it was altogether too challenging, and that even to talk became "impossible."

A friend shared something with me that gave me great insight into why we meet such inconsistency in people. Each person has a committee in their heads. Each moment behavior is dictated by inner (not necessarily conscious) decisions made by this committee. Each member of the committee has their own voice and agendas and priorities. And when the final decision is reached it may compromise a previous decision about a seemingly similar situation. It may not resemble a previous presumed reality closely, or at all. This can occur with complete unawareness that this has happened, consequently completely befuddling another person who this decision is being communicated to or who it may affect.

- - -

In life we register information through our senses. And being the mental animals that we are, we usually use the mind to evaluate this input. When we do this we have options, choices. What is it that is building our mind? Where do our opinions come from? What drives our decisions? First hand experience and information, or information reviewed and censured by a committee with an agenda? Or what blend?

- - -

Any conclusion by the committee will depend on when, under what circumstances, and for what reason a consensus is sought. Such a conclusion may be needed to base an action on or it may be to form an opinion.

Here are just a few examples of things that may affect the weight of the committee's voices and the final conclusion, opinion, or action that results:

- Is there a matter of physical survival at hand; be it real or imagined?

- Is a top priority in this moment to impress someone?

- Is there a personal history of opinion or action that doesn't want to be challenged?

- Is there a monetary element that might overshadow ideals that one holds?

- Are there ideals that carry so much weight that they suppress responding to a situation effectively?

If we listen for it, we will begin to hear the voices of the committee members in action. We can train ourselves to be aware of them. And as we begin to recognize the individual members and their individual agendas, we will gain insight into their sources. And also learn to recognize the issues that each member is concerned with and at what times or under what circumstances each committee member contributes their voice.

Also with each inner discussion among these committee members, the issue and the time and the circumstances will shape how loudly each member speaks out and how insistent each is at getting their own way and whether or not they will compromise readily. For every individual their committee members will be unique and the weight they carry in conference will be unique. Childhood experiences, family concerns, health issues and even such things as self image and other pressures put on us by society, friends, family, or self all have a voice.

One other thing that will certainly influence the final outcome is whether in past similar situations, the final decree of the committee lead to a successful or pleasurable outcome or not. Perhaps things have changed enough in one's life so that a choice that failed before will probably succeed now, but there will likely be a committee member who will lobby against taking similar action as before.

- - -

I was feeling anger towards a lover. We were both picking at each other over style concerns. I was disappointed in myself for letting style come between us and ahead of love. This from my journals:

> Though I didn't and really don't now feel it, exactly, it sure seems like another layer of the abandoned boy theme. I still have a voice picking on her for style in my head. I can still hear it as I write this. And that committee member is pouting and throwing a temper tantrum. It's a quiet voice but it's not going to go down so easily, I guess. And I admitted to myself that yes, I blamed over style and that's not good. But even as I write this I hear another voice, this one defending me with pride, "don't back down - blame someone else".

- - -

I'm often disturbed by how easily and effortlessly we glide along in life on a trail of psychological responses. Events compel psychology (That's important. Compel; not cause.) and that psychology surfaces at some later time and off we go in some purely Pavlovian determined direction.

We all have histories and it's not unusual to expect similar results form similar actions. We all have patterns that are innate to us; a style that is unique to us as souls in our bodies in this life. And it's only natural and often helpful that we have learned how to make the best choices for our well-being. But are we making the best choices for our well-being? Are we really being a fair witness or is our mind being made up for us out of awareness by the committee? We have our own ways, but I would suggest that much of what we believe (the committee's final decision) to be our limitations, are not. What we consider to be "me" is not as fixed as one might think. We have free will.

The more in touch we become with our committee members and the more closely we listen in, the better able we will be to help them grow out of being angrily reactionary or pouting or screaming and seeking to control and dominate the group's decision. And the better able we will be to help the whole committee mature and grow in integrity. The trick is to be present at the committee meetings and to take your rightful place at the head of the table.

- - -

Finally, these are some of the committee members that it occurs to me might be contributors to my decision making, personal tastes, prejudices and ultimately action taken, either upon the outside world or shaping my personality:

## Themes

- I want sex and now under any terms
- I want sex with love and romance
- I want to play hooky
- I want to be responsible and take care of things
- I want to be creative
- I want to it to be perfect – anything less isn't worth it
- I need to make money – I must survive
- I want to make money but under my terms – I must be comfortable
- I want to fit in with people; act in socially acceptable ways
- I must be myself; act as I will regardless of what people think

Each person will have their own unique committee with each member having its own relevance to their life and its individual niche in the pecking order of their committee as a whole. Think of the recurring patterns of your life and the choices of your personality and seek to observe and recognize the voices of your own committee members. Consciously become a participant.

- - -

One last thought. Seek to be aware of where each of the committee members is getting their information. Is it from personal experience? Is it from ideas or is it from sensory input? And maybe most importantly, is the information from other people things you haven't actually had experience with but are believing because you "learned" it? It is easy to give a lot of weight to anyone you deem to be an expert or qualified. Be careful or you might find that you have a committee member who is not even part of your home team.

# Consumer Consciousness

The level of attaining and consuming and holding onto physical possessions in our culture and especially in these modern times is an addiction and a distraction from other life issues. It is easier (easier in the smaller picture only) to focus on tangible things than to share with each other our real fears and joys. Change is necessary for the human spirit. We choose to experience change outside of ourselves instead of having to deal with it within. And so much effort and attention is put into not just the making of money but the juggling of money required to maintain particular possession standards. And to maintain the possessions themselves. They break down. Our "occupations" are just that. They, rather than living for life itself, take up our time.

- - -

The idea that we live in a culture obsessed with possessions and things is hardly new. But I see the attachment to possessing physical things as only the most superficial and crudest form of consumer consciousness. I believe that it is not unique to the recent centuries in the Western technological cultures or the current spread of ownable objects in the world. It is an extension of the 1st chakra need to claim turf and hold onto it against the world. This is where competition and jealousy and separation and, of course, war ultimately come from.

- - -

But our proclivity towards possessing and holding onto nonphysical things just as one would claim turf comes ultimately from even deeper than any 1st chakra survival consciousness. These are outward extensions of our karmicly compelled choices to hold onto nonphysical things because we aren't ready to let go to totalove; we still feel the need to take a stand against the world personally.

I see this manifested in relationships; particularly in intimate relationships. I have observed it in myself as I have lost a lover to her choice to not be as close to me as she had been. I feel cheated and like somebody owes me something. And I want to "have."

From a journal entry, the continuing conflict between the forces of unity and separation:

> The challenge of being at peace with myself amidst the head trips regarding hoped for futures with and the longing for Lori has compelled me to draw on my wisdom.
>
> The fact that I was feeling so solid within before (which created the space for her to come into my life in the first place) has compelled me to try and not lose the power that has been drawing in such beauty, amidst the drama of the physical world's separating and isolating influences.
>
> It's like a consumer mentality. Such and such desirable happens and you act like you own it (or them) now. If it goes away or changes, how dare that be taken from me.

- - -

Consumer consciousness can be related to things, people, or even conditions; even such things as the weather or a long line in the store. It's all too easy to forget that it is all a flow made up of all the participants and we just have to accept the small piece of the whole we are sharing in at any one moment. We must try and maintain grace and work on allowing the dynamics and not buy into the hoax of feeling we should own such moments in time.

- - -

I have often marveled at the appeal of Ronald Reagan and his happy-go-lucky superficiality; his epitomizing the American Dream. Einstein once said, "Everything should be made as simple as possible but not simpler." The Reagan mentality (and that of his huge following) gains its strength from its blindness to the complexity of the human condition and instead reduces everything to manageable proportions with only denial, self deceit and the suppression of conflicting evidence necessary. This is a case of making things simpler than possible. At least simpler than what is necessary if you want to function instead of decay. This mentality promotes consumption in its most wasteful way.

At times I have looked at people who, in my opinion, were behaving badly and thought of the expression "behaving like children." But that's not fair so I came up with the idea of "indoctrinated children." Unlike the natural beauty of content children, indoctrinated children fight over consumer products and the right of selfish freedom; indoctrinated into the cultural paradigm of individual stockpiling.

This leads to an unhealthy form of competitiveness and the belief that if we work hard enough we can get ahead. The problem is that ahead in this case means ahead of others and as we rise in this kind of competitive world, somebody always has to pay the price and if we want a piece of the action it will need be done at the expense of someone enslaved or downtrodden somewhere.

The paradigm of accumulation as an ideal must be blown apart. Not that having anything is bad but the obsession with it and the prioritizing of consumption must give way to a value based consciousness.

- - -

In this world of G.D.P. (gross domestic product) measuring the productiveness of countries, which seems to conflate production and well being, there has been an alternative idea from the small Himalayan kingdom of Bhutan. In 1972, Bhutan's new leader, King Jigme Singye Wangchuck, decided that in line with their Buddhist spiritual values they needed a different measure than that of western material values. He decided that the measure should be the G.N.H., or gross national happiness. Happiness as the goal to be achieved through development as opposed to development as a means to having more. To this end the king instituted policies and took efforts so that prosperity would be shared across society and that it was balanced against preserving cultural traditions and protecting the environment.

It is only values and other non-possessable "things" that can guide us through the great problems of the world and help foster well being, security and happiness.

- - -

And finally, this journal entry is a good example of me wanting to escape because things had changed. I wanted to own the stability. Struggling with conflicting desires and with my questions about life style and place; with community choices and with climate preferences:

I had a realization while walking today. It seems important and I hope I can profit from recognizing it.

The rhythm I had for the month in California before I came up north into the winter is gone. At least its outward appearance and probably both what ways I was given gifts and how I recognize the gifts I was given. I may have, discover, recognize, or settle into another rhythm but that previous particular phase is gone. So many conditions have changed. Both externally and how I perceive things. I realize it would be destructive and wasteful to seek that same rhythm or lament its passing. Now I must simply try and live what grace I can.

Physical things come and go. People come and go. Creature comforts come and go. Values and sharing and love prevail if you make room for them. They are our birthright and inviolable. Seek to cultivate them.

## True Efficiency

The idea of efficiency has become extremely distorted. In this rat race world, efficiency seems to have come to mean several things which I would say are very shallow minded gauges of true efficiency.

One main measure is time – clock time. Faster is better, often with little regard to quality. Faster, whether it is faster that something is produced or faster that we get somewhere or faster that we can get something done so that we can get on to something else. Which, of course, will also have to be done as fast as possible to get on to something else. That's efficiency.

- - -

When I lived in Hawaii I worked as a checker in a health food store.

Another checker harassed me for being slow and taking too much time with the customers, which really disturbed me.

So I got to thinking, why are people in such a hurry? It seemed clear to me that it's because what they're doing isn't enjoyable. Or it is not felt fully enough and appreciated or valued enough. It's that simple.

Maybe at the store we should have had one line for people who want to chat amongst each other and with farmer Brown while they buy their goods at the market and another line for those people who want to be processed like the numbers on their credit cards, "efficiently," so they can get going and get more done.

Maybe the difference is between the goals of getting things "done." Over and done. Or "doing." Enjoying the process; feeling good along the way. Just what is the point of getting more things done, if none of those things are enjoyable.

I am sure that here someone could argue that some things are rushed so as to have more time for things that are more enjoyable. There is some truth to that but I would say that if that is the case then the overall lifestyle and choices of activities needs to be questioned. And I would also say that to be engaged in a balancing act of rushing through unenjoyable events to get to enjoyable events has a pitfall. The rushing creates stress which will often carry over to the times when we choose to slow down.

- - -

As well as faster, bigger and more are also often thought to be equated with efficiency and productiveness. If one is good, two must be better. If one boogawatt of power production will provide our community well, then certainly two will make life even better and/or easier. I think it is all too often that bigger and more are simply assumed to be desirable and are the goals, and how much bigger and how much more indicate efficiency.

- - -

True efficiency must take in to account all factors. One factor is the consumption of material and energy and everything involved in their being harnessed for whatever is wanting to be accomplished. Another factor is the well-being of all people whose lives are touched by whatever is being done. Another would be the impact of the act or event itself on the person who is supposed to be benefitting from it; not just on the surface if it gets something done but is there value and appreciation. It's like I could work 4 hours doing something I don't enjoy and get paid $80 and then go and spend that money plus $20 out of my pocket to buy a piece of furniture or I could spend that same $20 on materials and spend 8 hours in the shop whistling while I work and build that piece of furniture. Would that be inefficient to spend twice as much time or would the satisfaction of a job well done and the feeling and residual energy of having spent such a pleasant day constitute true efficiency?

Certainly that is for each individual to decide. In this life there is bound to be undesirable things that must be done and choices to be made. But I think one should always look at the whole to decide which route to take.

The same question might be applied to gift giving; Christmas gifts, for example. I could do all my shopping in one day or I might to choose to chip away at several craft projects over a period of weeks and give home-made gifts. The appreciation of the receiver of the gifts and overall warmth of the experience must be considered in calculating the true efficiency.

- - -

I think a little needs to be said here about these times, often referred to as "the information age." The efficiency of the computer is unparalleled. Or is it?

As far as efficiency goes, I believe the experience of going to and spending time at the library to study something or maybe being compelled to try an experiment yourself to get an answer or needing help from friends or a teacher may offer much more than the slick ability of a computer to seek out and isolate the intended item.

I know my life would have been gaunt had the accidents, the wrong turns, and the serendipitous encounters been replaced by the efficiency of targeting a sought out piece of information on a computer. Not to mention that the openness of the mind required to deal with those wrong turns and mistakes offers so much more.

The idea that you can get more information from a zillion items of verbal information coming down a wire than you can, say, from the same amount of time spent looking at a stump decaying in the woods, is ludicrous.

- - -

One of the narratives in politics these days is that now is not the time to spend money on such things as health care as a community responsibility or to invest in new approaches to help the environment; during these hard times we need to stick with the status quo. This is a great example of fragmented shortsighted thinking. While the money machines and the interests of the greedy (and the masses who blindly get behind the program) have foisted themselves and their factories on the world for the dollar made today, no care has been taken to see if they would fit; if the earth could accommodate them. As time goes along the manifestations of these poorly conceived ideas get more and more out of balance. Shortsightedness just leads to forever having to rework that which is out of balance in a patchwork fashion in an attempt to forestall its collapse. This is not efficient. It is upside down.

More on the dollar made today. On a personal level, accumulating money and the leverage it gives us in life make the amount of money we have and saving on bargain purchases seem desirable. It's not that simple. There are many side issues around making more and more money and spending money superficially efficiently that affect the big picture which will come back to haunt us. It is often the case that the ways in which money is made and that which is involved in a "growing" economy has consequences. It is often overlooked that beyond the obvious value of having more money left over today, the money you have may be worth less tomorrow because of your actions. In a similar vein it is extremely inefficient to put your money in a bank, regardless of the dollar made today that they promise you, if that bank is using your money to make people's lives miserable and reduce the quality of life for all of us.

Doing the right thing is always more efficient. There are, of course, times, in a physical world and a manifest world that is out of balance, when less than the most truly efficient routes must be taken back to balance and harmony. But all less efficient steps taken must be acknowledged as such and be taken in awareness.

- - -

I have been eating as much organic food as I can for many decades now. Especially early on, before it became more in vogue, I would have friends say, "yeah, but it's so expensive." My answer was simple. You can pay a little extra for organic food now or you can pay a lot more for doctors later. And this is not to mention one's well-being in the meantime. And this well-being goes beyond just your health, but includes what you have contributed to the public welfare by not contributing to the poisoning of the earth.

- - -

To seek real efficiency and real value, the bigger picture must always be consulted. Also the soul. If some end is achieved faster or cheaper, is that more efficient if it is at the expense of our sensitivities? We are done of the task sooner but have less spirit with which to carry on.

Efficiency must be, by definition, that which is the best for the balance and the harmony of the whole. Good feelings, pleasurable feelings and compatibility must be measures of efficiency. Justice must be taken into account. Values and ideals must be factored in. With true efficiency ease instead of dis-ease will prevail.

# Tourist in Life Concept

Once when I was in the airport in London, I was watching the passengers coming off a plane. Among them was a pretty sizable group of Texans. (I'm guessing but the accent and the 10 gallon hats suggested that to me.) They rambled into the airport and instead of any sort of wonder about being in a new or foreign place or any sort of checking out the environment to gauge how people behaved, they just brought Texas with them and were loud and, I thought, quite insensitive.

During my travels I have noted that there is a big distinction between tourists and travelers. Travelers are simply moving among other fellow earth inhabitants of various cultures in this multi-faceted world, adjusting to their surroundings and consequently sharing and contributing to wherever they are and whoever they are with. They are experiencing and learning and growing personally as well. Tourists, on the other hand, never shuck their home persona or their home paradigms, blundering coarsely along contributing little more than money. Certainly the difference between travelers and tourists is not absolute, but I do notice the distinction generally.

- - -

People who have known me are often amazed by how deeply affected I am by a book or a movie or music. There have been times when I have felt such a deep sensitivity and have felt misunderstood. It occurred to me that the concept of the tourist could be applied in so many other ways than just when traveling.

# Themes

People are, it seems to me, also tourists in art and tourists in so much that they do. When involved in something or experiencing something, they don't shuck their selves in order to truly experience.

When you read a book, is it just a story or do you allow it to reach you and to affect you? When you listen to music is time altered as it becomes an adventure? Or when you look at a painting is it just a picture or can you go into it? An expression that became popularized in the sixties, which probably sprung from the focus and submersion in the moment that was characteristic of the times as well as being enhanced by psychedelic drugs, was "get into it." Yeah, don't just observe. Get into it; participate.

Another example would be to look at what level people participate with nature when they go camping. Are they tourists in nature, bringing along all the comforts of home, smelling the fresh air, to be sure, but not really submitting themselves enough to really be taking part in nature? Or is the camping trip intended to be an adventure in nature with a real choice to allow yourself to be vulnerable to some extent to really feel what it is like there? I would suggest that if you go beyond being the tourist in nature that even that fresh air would take on a new level of richness.

I wrote "vulnerable" above and I think this is maybe the real issue. The tourist experiences with trepidation and is cautious about allowing themselves to be too out of control. Standardized food choices and standardized accommodations are maintained. It is from inside this safety net that they view or look "at" their surroundings. In situations where people leave the routine, they tend to take their "down pat" selves with them as insulation against being affected and consequently challenged.

--–

I would go even further and apply this to such things as relationships. When you are with others or with a lover, do you really let yourself into it? Are you willing to be vulnerable in order to fully experience? Or do you seek to maintain your own ways to insure that you won't have to change too much or accommodate too much?

--–

There is one pattern for me in my life that has been frustrating, even though I see it as a strength. I often find it very difficult to get into people's lives. I'm often awkward and uncertain. But once I'm in, I'm relaxed and get along well and it's easy. With women in particular something that has happened a lot is that we come together when one or the other of us is about to leave, has just arrived, or is traveling.

But it's not just traveling; I've noticed how easily I enter during vulnerable moments. When people are tough and really have their thing down I find it so much harder and if I do get in, I find it less than satisfying. When I or a woman are moving, the everyday life thread, the profession, career, patterns, agenda are suspended or loose and I can enter. I've watched myself gain confidence and flirt and move closer; move in to a nice sharing when I sense that.

It fits with the idea about being a tourist in love. Since I don't desire being a tourist in love and really can't be that way, if I don't see a way in, and sense that she just wants me to touch her on the outside, I don't make the adjustments necessary to stay in the "do you come here often?" mode for very long and that's that.

## Themes

- - -

This from my journals:

> I've always differentiated between tourists and travelers. Tourists being, well.... you know, .... sightseers, outsiders taking pictures and seeing it as if it were a picture - 2 dimensional; going home virtually unchanged. Travelers being fully alive where they are, still living their life, being affected by their environment; knowing and expecting they will be changed by their experiences - full 3 dimensional involvement. Yes, that fits too with my tourist in love, or tourist in nature thoughts. I want to be a traveler in love. Open up the threads of our lives, let our loves intermingle and let's travel.

I would go further and suggest that this concept could even be applied to personal reflection and introspection. When your senses perceive something and convey it to you, is it immediately compartmentalized or do you allow yourself to accept it out of predetermined programming and allow yourself to be an adventurer in the moment?

- - -

When I was younger and lived in the Pacific Northwest, I would often go out and play sports on wet playfields with friends. Initially I would be reserved about getting wet and muddy. I would avoid falling or diving for a catch. But sooner or later it would happen anyway. Once I was wet and muddy, it all opened up. That's when the fun began.

- - -

A ship is safe as long as it stays in port, but that's not what ships are built for. Leave the port, leave the hotel, leave your self, leave the way it's always been. Allow the adventure in. Let yourself be taken by the river of unchartered experience and participate.

## True Love

Once, when listening to the classical station on the radio, the announcer read a quote from a musician who said the most important part of the music is the listener: "We're all trying to reach the listener." Woah, hold on there! I think the finest music is made when the musicians play for themselves. In a similar vein questions about self focus vs. community came into my mind and it seemed so clear. There is no conflict. How would our body function if the liver was trying to perform for some other part of the body and taking its attention away from its task at hand. The key is to be the best you can be and allow others that for themselves. And when actions bring beings into close (recognizable) contact, then bring in awareness and communication toward recognizing each other's roles toward the best functioning (harmony).

The beauty of it is that as you remain your own organ, the smoother you all function, and the more easily energy can flow through and among you. And with this energy comes the feeling of oneness and union and well-being; this feeling is what we all yearn for. Example: I sure don't want to be (or own) a woman's belly, or breast, or voice, or movement. What am I going to do with that? I want what/who she is when she is as much as she can be of all of what she is. I want to feel the velvet that comes from allowing each other to flow. Any effort towards the other is best only to facilitate the other's opening to their own way.

Take it as far as you want. Any way you look at it, it's by increasing each participant's ability to function smoothly, happily, effectively, that we all reap the benefits.

This is True Love.

- - -

I mentioned to a friend once about how being an individualist is part of the American creed. He seemed very cautious, almost afraid of individuality. He commented, questioning whether it is good, being self oriented and away from the whole.

I got to thinking, how would it be if a drop in the ocean refused to evaporate. "I feel it to evaporate. The temperature is right, the pressure is right. But I'm gonna stay here with you guys. I can't go off and do my own thing."

The rivers would dry up and ocean would stagnate.

It seems paradoxical, but to move freely with our own influences as parts of the whole is what really brings beauty and unity to the whole.

Make no mistake about it. Togetherness because of fear, intimidation, or for purely philosophical reasons is not unity. And certainly not if it requires compromise of self or personal values.

- - -

I once encountered a book titled: Must I Change Who I Am To Be Loved By You? The answer is so obvious. Absolutely. All beings must change who and what they are to be alive. Love is change. Love is motion. What's important, though, is that the changing is done organically and dynamically as part of the relationship and as part of each individual's growth; not in order to comply with one or the other's idea of what form the relationship should ultimately take.

I think that describes well the problem I have had in some relationships. I experienced a lot of pain because I tried to match energy with women who needed validation for who they were statically; not for their motion.

Sure, I guess, in the purest sense of the word love, I can love them too; I can love you if you don't change, but not in the sense of being together in an intimate relationship.

And it's not just me. Any two beings that are together, to validate or because of validating their staticness are going to encounter functioning problems.

I can think right off of some of my friends' relationships that I have observed that were burdened by movement problems because change scared them rather than excited them.

I have always recognized that I need movement and change in relationships. I gave away my power often, thinking if I didn't yield to a status quo, I'd lose something I needed. Now, it's just too clear to me that the value in a relationship that resists the dance of the currents and the impulses of life can't compare to a state, single or coupled, that is free to flow and move and change.

- - -

There is a form of "meditation" that, rather than seeking God or some higher spiritual state, focuses on being aware of yourself, your own energy, and coming back home to feel solid and complete within yourself, in order to function more clearly and effectively.

There was a time when a couple of friends and I had done such a meditation and afterwards we were all aware of how crystal clear everything looked. And I began to wonder if that's also why at times women I have been with have looked so good to me when I was feeling very individual, very me. How much better they looked than when I was losing myself in us.

Certainly it seems that it's been true in my love life that lovers look better when I've done some activity that is for me. What a beautiful paradox and lesson for lovers. There's such a compulsion, almost guilt driven, that we should lose ourselves in each other to attain unity. And going even so far as to think that if we don't, then maybe we don't really care. But by remaining separate we retain our ability to sense, to feel, to see crystal clear, and to function creatively.

I really see now, how, for the most part, a really selfish "I don't feel like it now, tough" attitude can be healthy. The times of coming together will be of a higher quality. True love. Yes! That's what true love is. Loving because at that moment it's exactly what you want to be doing and you are doing it the way you feel like doing it.

And, perhaps, the measure of a relationship is how often true love happens; when both people are expressing love creatively and in their own ways simultaneously often enough to satisfy each other.

And I guess that need (to be satisfied) would always be in flux; paradoxically becoming less with the knowing that the other desires to share their true love with you. Which, of course, makes it easier when it's less demanding.

It's the opposite of the viscous circle!

- - -

This entry from my journals:

> The last couple of days I've been feeling it to be lovers with a woman and feeling really impersonal about it. Keith has said a few times how he wants a woman "for a while" and it seemed so impersonal and kind of weird to me. But now I understand. It is a paradox, really, that in a way that is really an ultimate state and a compliment. It's like two people can love so much that the giving doesn't require any particular response or any particular niche for the other person to fit into or prove anything in order to love. Just love, as freely as they are capable, share, and know it is just that.

- - -

And the true love theme wouldn't be complete without:

## Free Love

While playing some romantic 60's songs, I was thinking about my pain and loneliness and my attachment to certain women in my life. I thought about the Prince Valiant and Lady in distress syndrome; about putting them on a pedestal and losing perspective; losing touch with all the elements that constitute objective reality. And how these things create conditions, really create the environment from which my feelings come, or perhaps through which they are filtered, shaped, and charged, coming from deeper within.

And what I came to is this: I believe that in a natural society with joyous, free, spontaneous, creative people, people would receive enough loving. Men and women would flirt, play, and come together easily. In between, or perhaps among, magical relationships of duration, men and women could kiss, could stroke each other, could praise each other, and could make love to each other. With clarity and good intentions various levels of closeness happen naturally.

I feel that if one always knew that loving and appreciation and touch and sex weren't far away, that we wouldn't distort our perceptions to satisfy our need to feel loved or to pretend anybody is more or other than they are.

Of course, this requires participation. Both with each other and with ourselves.

Not having attachments doesn't mean not having commitments.

Without having all your eggs in one basket you can love each other for what you offer in real functional life - not fantasies.

So.... I believe in this. And why doesn't this happen? Very few people are ready for this, which is simply to say they can't imagine it. I can. And I feel in light of this, that finding and/or creating a community or circle of people who desire this is very important to me.

Not a frivolous free love sex society, but a commitment to owning our feelings and owning our emotions. Also a climate where people feel safe to take emotional risks.

True loving.

Themes

# Life Between and Behind the Lines

While listening to the Doors I was listening to a guitar solo and was thinking of how descriptive the 60's expressions were. "Get into it" is kind of cliché, but that's what I was doing with the guitar solo. I was getting into it. Kinda getting smaller, going into slow motion and microscope size and going inside, until the parts got bigger compared to me.

These lyrics are from the poem "The Movie" on the Doors album "American Prayer":

The program for this evening is not new

You've seen this entertainment through and through

You've seen your birth your life and death

You might recall all of the rest

Did you have a good world when you died?

Enough to base a movie on?

There is something there - an attitude - that is really important. And that is that the real history of the world is lurking between the headlines and the deadlines. Like the essences that are so hard to grasp and that deny form and that are so important and that we belittle because we want, we desperately need to associate with things we can hold on to. Yes, we do all have lives that contain enough to base a movie on. And maybe our task in life is to recognize and validate the guts of our life that just doesn't get much press but has

59

tremendous value. It almost seems to me that finding that could be the key to happiness.

- - -

Get into it. Get past the cliché. Really get into it. Get inside. Slow time down and get in step with whatever you are doing, seeing, hearing, feeling, smelling, touching, or imagining. And validate it all. Be in the center of your life.

- - -

My sophomore year in high school I had an English teacher who had a recurring class discussion theme that was the question, "What is a full life?" There we were, a bunch of 16 year olds who he'd gotten to start thinking about and talking about what we thought a full life was. Can a 16 year old rightly reflect on a full life? Why not. Life is doing; not done.

In today's world especially, I would say, there is pressure to have some sort of notoriety; to do and accomplish things that you can put in your life résumé or post on your personal bulletin board. And there seems to be certain traditional societal standards that define those things that we give recognition for when seen posted by others.

- - -

There has, I think, been some awareness of and improvement regarding this on some levels. For example more has been written in recent years about history from the viewpoint of everyone involved; not just the winners and those with the coarse leverage to effect outcomes of events; not just the (mostly) men who were on the front lines, at least the apparent front lines, making the most noise. But it needs to go further than just giving praise to the less than famous people. We need more validation for the much subtler influences that shape life.

Yes, history is not so simple as a series of acts that you can put your finger on; those acts that lead to laws, leaders, and lands changing in one event or at one distinct moment. There is always a fabulous, multidimensional, rich tapestry of underlying influences.

If some person is famous for something they said, did, discovered, or invented, it would be nice to be able to look back and into their life and see what a spouse might have said or shared with them or what kind of state of mind they were in because of their children. The point is that this is really where the stuff of life and the stuff that shapes our lives come from. Between the lines. And somehow, recognizing the thread is important. Not so much recognizing it in your head as something you can label but recognizing it as the real substance of life.

- - -

The 1967 movie Camelot affects me deeply each time I see it. King Arthur's vision of a new order: not Might makes Right, but Might for Right. And a Round Table. Equals. But as real life takes place, dreams and ideals are challenged by history's weight. Even as King Arthur himself was willing to allow and forgive and to let his heart guide him, the pressures from without were too much.

(If you still have yet to see the movie and don't want some of the essence of the movie and a scene at the end given away don't read this. Rent the movie, watch it, then read this.)

In the end sides are taken and preparation is made for war. A young boy, maybe 11 or 12 years old, has stowed away with the soldiers and reveals himself to King Arthur. He wants to join the battle that is expected at daybreak. The failure of the dream of Camelot and the reverting to the old ways of solving conflict is weighing heavily on Arthur. But in the boy he sees hope; the hope of the future. Yes. There will come a time. Arthur tells him that fighting for Right is not what it's about. He tells the boy to go back and take with him the vision of Camelot as it is in its ideal. And to grow tall and straight and to live for that. He sends him off into the pre-dawn mist and tells him, "Run, boy, run! Behind the lines. Yes. Go back and keep the dream of Camelot alive. Run, boy, run. Behind the lines!"

Yes. Behind the lines. While all the mayhem and hoopla and futile destruction takes place, run.... behind the lines. And keep the dream alive.

- - -

Reading the Free Press, an alternative newspaper, one day, I really sensed that behind the lines the movement is of such a higher quality. The enlightenment and hopefully the subsequent appropriate enacting is so much deeper and broader. It's not just the apparent event, not the events that get distilled into simple manageable situations that can now be spoken of and worked on, but it's the essence of issues and the unifying principles which is where the guts of movement and change really is.

This entry from my journals:

> Last night I was feeling pretty low. Grim, I guess you could say. As I laid down in bed I became

aware of a part of myself, behind the lines, kinda bopping and groovin' to music; being silly and kinda free. Nice to see and realize those feelings are really a part of me; really of part of the whole me.

What do we give press to within ourselves? Is it the struggles that make good news and are easily tapped and accessible? Or is it that which is happening behind the lines of our outer personality? This is where the lodes and loads of gold lie.

## Karma and Grace

Every choice is karma.
Every choice is group mind.
Every choice is the earth's aura - the ether.

- - -

There was a time when I was living in the country outside of Santa Cruz, California. It was my habit to work in my outdoor shop at home during the morning and early afternoon. An interesting thing that seemed to have much to do with my waking in and being surrounded by only nature for the first half of the day was that often when I went to town and first saw people at a distance from my car, I saw them as animated shells and saw the choice of each individual to inhabit their own particular handicap; each having brought that with them or actually as them.

I would often be aware of and sense the field of energy around people that is the matrix that protects, no, that holds them to the experiences they have. Like, it's amazing that we don't all have accidents, stub toes, step on nails, etc. much more often. Accidents and events don't just happen. I was "seeing" the field that we each have, somehow linking our bodies to our design. And this is one aspect of the package that we bring into this life as our karma.

- - -

While traveling in Austria, I was offered a place to stay after offering to help an older woman struggling with a bit of carpentry on her house. While there, at one point, she asked about my beliefs. I said I talked to God and to angels, but didn't believe in God as a man. It was conforming with natural law. She agreed.

I explained also how I felt, like the Bible says, we can ask and we shall receive. We can look for signs and not repeat mistakes.

She said she was afraid of planes and I explained that I used to be, but now I look at the people waiting to board the plane and the energy and ask if these people are going to die today. When I get the answer no, I feel safe.

It is similar to seeing that matrix. There are no flat out victims who are in the wrong place at the wrong time. There are choices to live what we need to in order to learn what we need to.

- - -

In life there are always repeating patterns; opportunities to get it right. The thing is to make those loops spiral. Tape loops that just replay don't resolve karma.

There have been times when I have had feelings that I'm finally fed up and I'm seeking a missing link in myself. I've begun to suspect that this link is in the way of my honesty, purity, and true wholesomeness. I have felt that it goes back to patterns that are deep in the past. I've felt like I'm chickening out on my power.

The search for the missing link is the search for whatever it is that it takes to make the process spiral and not loops.

- - -

I had this realization during a time of extraordinary rhythm in my life. From my journals:

> I have sometimes wondered where my rewards are and after doing good deeds have wondered how

or when I would get rewarded. I have been many many times the good Samaritan, but feel that I have reaped very few rewards for it. Where is my good karma? What I realized is that that way of looking for rewards has been transcended. I now feel aware that free of history and living in unity, events that might have been labeled successes or failures or might have been considered rewards are simply all part of the same matrix. And as far as the question, where is my good karma? It is not to be found as an end result. The more I live in unity, the more I am one with events and with my fellow beings, then what might have been seen as rewards before are now simply recognized as facets of what I think of as "my life."

Two years later, during a time when I felt that my faith was very high and that my acts were part of a spiritual reality which I all too often forget (no, not forget intellectually; forget in the core of my being, while being swept along in daily life surrounded by the paradigm of hard work for hard results) I was aware of a similar cosmic reality.

I observed how my acts of kindness, my "good karma" acts seemed to be supporting my ether, as it were. Often, in the past, when I'd wondered where the repayment was, there was an attitude of cynicism and separation. Like, "pay up universe."

Imagine raising a kid that way. "Let's see if you can do this. I'll bet you can't," along with the cynical vibe. Pretty bad.

But what I was feeling was not a "re-action" from the universe, rather I was seeing my acts resulting in good feelings in me that supported my ability to project myself such that I encountered a kind world.

It's so subtle, but it seems like a curious paradoxical place of power that at once is life created by me and life simply lived and participated in by me.

- - -

Everything you do or think or intend becomes a part of you, as well as a part of the whole; the god we all are. The earth is a place of doing; it's where doing really matters. That's really the whole point. Hard physical doing creates results that are often irreversible. It could be physical harm or it could be to set a course of action rolling that will lead to a change for the worse. Such doing, such actions create karma. Which means it's not consequence free for the doer.

Thoughts and intentions do have consequences, within and without, but in a less dramatic sense. Thoughts and intentions affect the ether and they can be felt as vibrations, like perhaps the mood in a room or at a gathering of folks. But in this realm, subtler than the hard physical doing, there is a lot of room to change your vibrations, and "make good" without apparent long term consequences.

In any case, acts out of harmony indicate that the doer is not in harmony within themselves, and therefore they must in some way be thrust again into a situation to get it right.

One of the great misunderstandings about karma, however, is that it is all about what we do to others; it is also what we do to ourselves. When we hurt others, we have chosen the low road and stepped off of the high road to heaven. It is our own well being that is compromised. The act out of harmony causes tension, affects your blood flow and pressure and adds friction to the full energetic system that you are. It is awkwardness where there should be ease. It is heavy where there should be light. And it is an entanglement of the future and the past where there should be free sailing.

- - -

Personally, I use the words "bad karma" and "good karma", but mostly as convenience to simplify and to avoid going into the nuances. And, although there are many nuances, there is some truth to the concept of and really no harm in most of the time just thinking of karma as good or bad. However, considering the nuances, there really is no "bad" karma. Bad karma compels us to be thrust into situations where we must learn a lesson that we had an opportunity to learn and failed, so that we have another chance. In that sense it's good. It's bad in the sense that it may be very undesirable or uncomfortable. It often involves such things as having to walk a mile in the shoes, so to speak, of another being that was hurt by our actions.

And as far as "good" karma goes, I would say good karma is when we act in such a way that it supports, encourages, and helps bring about unity, both for ourselves within and consequently for the whole and the greater good and health of the whole. It is harmonious. Good karma doesn't compel repetition of lessons to be learned, rather it is "rewarded" by ease, harmony, and good feelings. And this is what I call grace.

I used the word "compel" in describing bad karma. Somehow the universe, with us in complicity, compels us to learn somehow the lesson failed to be learned before. In grace, we play a more active role in the choices of future situations we will find ourselves in along our path.

Each time we return to earth physically for another sojourn, we return with "good" and "bad" karma. As we refine our self and become more in harmony, grace tends to play a bigger role and we are less compelled and choose more ease. The lessons become gentler.

- - -

Having said what I said above about being compelled to learn the lessons we failed before, I would like to add that I believe it doesn't necessarily have to be a long trudging road as we refine ourselves. I believe that a lifetime of karma can be erased with a thought. I haven't seen much evidence of that on such a scale but I have experienced within myself and observed in others the ability to let go to harmony, superseding something that might have compelled a karmic response. Though it does seem to be more in our nature to struggle and to let go of small pieces of our baggage a little at a time I do not believe there is a rule that we have to struggle. Redemption is a powerful tool.

- - -

Finally, I can't feel that I'm done with the karma and grace theme without addressing the death penalty.

The death penalty is first of all just plain barbaric. The only reason for the death penalty is for revenge. Fact of the matter is that those who wish it, support it, or do it, and especially those who revel in it, incur a great deal of heavy karma.

Among other things, one thing the death penalty does is that it denies the person a chance to redeem themselves, no matter what crime they have committed. If allowed to live, they are granted the opportunity to find the place where they were out of harmony and to come to a place within themselves where they can heal that aspect of their karma. Redemption is not an act done so you can say I did public service or did time and paid my dues and now I'm cleansed. It is something more of the heart and soul. Coming to a place of real knowing within. There are no guarantees that any individual will do this but when a person is denied this opportunity, it isn't just bad for them, it hurts everyone. It leaves an open wound and we all will pay in some way for that lost opportunity to have that wound healed.

One of my favorite themes in the original Star Trek series was redemption and belligerent beings returning to the fold. There were many episodes in which warring people (I say people for simplicity's sake) or people who had done great harm or committed heinous acts were forgiven in the end. Out in space Kirk was not forced to obey a law written in stone; he was allowed his judgment. And many who committed "criminal" acts weren't punished once it was clear that misunderstandings and injustices were recognized and those who had committed the misdeeds had made peace within and now felt it to be one with the community. Kirk was able to recognize the redemption and the opportunity to welcome a new friend and confidently allowed these people a chance to start over on a new higher path.

Of course that was fiction and very idealistic but still, I believe, something for us, both personally and as a society, to strive for as much as we can.

# The Golden Rule Dilemma

Do unto others as you would have them do unto you. It sounds simple enough, on the surface. I have respected it as a truly admirable cornerstone of the best of the Christian tenets. Then it occurred to me that it has really been a player in many of the dilemmas I have faced. And it is, in its purest essence, really very controversial.

I have looked into the golden rule equivalent in other religions. They all have their own versions but most are similar. Some take a negative approach. Don't do unto others what you would not have them do unto you. It seemed to me, based on the translations and realizing that they are of other cultures, to the best of my understanding, that they are all equally oversimplified and controversial.

Following are some thoughts relative to this.

- - -

I want to be able to expect a lot from people and I put it on friends.

In the purest sense of doing to others what you would have them do to you, I have often disturbed and enraged people, because I would have people challenge me, tell me how they see it and be open and forward.

For example, I do wish my friends could and would be happy. But I think for me, how I wish it or show it is so different. It seems to me that mostly when people wish happiness on or for friends, it is a kind of pure, simple, wish. Just be happy. I think that is hard for me to do in a similar manner because invariably I see so much that I feel they need to undo before they can be happy and that undoing becomes part of the wish; part of my best intentions' wish for them. Maybe they could even be what they call happy but it's hard for me to wish that on them. The dilemma here is that what I would wish that they would do unto me is to challenge me to face issues in order to be happy. I would wish that they would want to help me change. Yet if I do that unto them, without explicit permission, more often than not it would be unwanted.

Interesting question. Should one recognize others' resistance and be honest only to a point, staying in realms comfortable to them, allowing, or should one really do unto others?

So, let me offer this addition to the golden rule. It is the way in which you are true and straight in doing unto others. Are you harsh or soft; attacking or cultivating? Maybe the "do" unto others is the problem. Maybe it should be more like "while doing unto others be sure to nurture them as you would want to be nurtured."

- - -

In the Evil theme I talked about the big discussion that I had with a couple of people I knew about laws and licensing massage; they were defending required licenses and a small group of people's right to legislate their ethics and I was simply saying, what can be wrong with adults deciding to do anything peaceful together with no victims. They defended their view saying it wasn't the government who decided the rules; it was a group of massage therapists.

As far as their side goes, for all of their benevolent dictator attitude, were they also acting with the golden rule? Did they prefer being told by authorities what not to do, simplifying their lives? And therefore did they feel it was also in my best interest to be controlled, and doing unto me would be to control me? There is the rub.

- - -

At Harbin Hot Springs there is an area with a number of small decks for camping. When there once I had some tension with a woman on the next deck over about my taking over a deck that has some stuff on it but seemed to me to be unused; the few items seemed abandoned. She told me she didn't think I should use the deck. I suggested using the deck and graciously yielding it if someone were to show up saying it was theirs. She told me that was a really male pushy thing to do. She wanted Harbin security to ok the take over, which, of course, pushed my buttons.

Afterwards, it occurred to me that both of us had been using the golden rule.

With all good intent and hopes to ease the tension, I went back later and expressed to her my thoughts, suggested that we were both just doing what we thought was best, and about us both using the golden rule. She was grim and uptight and seemed to refuse to find any common ground we could come to.

I guess that was just an escalation of the first failing of the golden rule. For me, doing unto her was to attempt to make peace so we could live happily ever after. For her, doing unto others; what she would expect from me, was to leave it alone regardless of the unresolved tension. And to relegate the resolution to Authority.

A possible golden rule interpretation: maybe it's not the physical act, but the intention. If I do unto others it might be very disturbing. Perhaps instead temper, tailor the act to achieve my intent; an act they appreciate.

But that's tricky. That means I'm guessing about them.

- - -

Once I was thinking about pleasure and how it is so distorted in the world. How people get pleasure from things that hurt others or disturb others. A picture came to me of two people together affecting each other, each creating, imparting vibrations that bring pleasure to the other as well as themselves. But what about the sadist and masochist? This is where the golden rule breaks down big time.

The golden rule has to be modified somehow to call upon the people of the world to seek within for the goodness that wants all participants to share in the highest potential of pleasure and well being.

- - -

There was an article in a Peace Pilgrim Newsletter that told about a lawyer, inspired by Peace Pilgrim's book, Steps Toward Inner Peace, to work with other lawyers to mediate for the parties involved instead for fighting to win. He refers to the golden rule of dispute resolution: "Have it be your purpose to resolve the dispute rather than to gain advantage."

On a more etheric level the following is similar to this idea of not gaining advantage. I sometimes catch myself thinking unkind things about people. It came to me that there is a difference between thinking unkind thoughts and being aware of what's unpleasant or disturbing or distasteful. It's perfectly fine and even desirable to be aware of vibrations that feel unharmonious but it is something else altogether to be away from a situation and to continue to generate unkind thoughts or blame or judge. The latter binds everyone to a rigid psychic event. The former, being a proper use of awareness, then letting it go, can free us and allow all parties the psychic freedom we all need to improve ourselves and our lives.

This is a form of the golden rule for sure. And a pure one without catches.

- - -

In conclusion, I would say hear the words of the golden rule but modify it constantly and dynamically for each and every situation with the ultimate intent being to soften each others lives and nurture each other and promote equality and justice.

# Imagination

Regarding the romance I wanted in my life but seemed unable to have, a friend was getting on my case, telling me it was just that I didn't believe I could have it. I got angry. Angry being challenged with the responsibility of creating my own outward physical reality.

Later, reflecting on it, it came to me so clearly.

I believe I'm healthy. My imaginings of health are strong.

Part of me believes I can have women and sex. But my shadow side says no. And in this case, its imagining is stronger.

There have been times of confidence and times when I've been validated from without when I could easily imagine having a fruitful romantic life but when encountering a disappointment, I let my shadow imaginings take over. It was not a lack of imagining my desires fulfilled; just a stronger imagining of being unsuccessful in that area of life. When there were difficulties in a relationship either I was a victim (read, fell victim to my shadow imaginings) or I neatly avoided imagining my ability to play a strong active role in a failing relationship and know my power to imagine us changing and growing.

Looking back I see that during those times of happiness and satisfaction I had good opportunities, with the confidence and validation, to seek out the roots of and challenge my shadow imaginings. When things go well is when you really have opportunities to recreate your patterns.

- - -

That example is about me personally, but I think it is a good one, because I doubt that it is unique to me and because it is really just about the levels of imagining and their interplay.

This from my journals regarding a woman I desired:

> I was phantasizing us being together and her yielding to me. It was such a down energy. Why not imagine she might enjoy and desire loving me? In her own way and her own time. Since I can't control her anyway, this frees me of trying to manipulate her imaginings. Only that there's love out there and I can imagine my love might be desired. All I can expect is to be as close to someone or as compatible with someone as their imaginings allows them to be with me.

We all have karma and bring tendencies into each life, but they are only tendencies. It's not that we are forever affected by such influences and consequently live our lives as we do. It is simply that we; our faith, our positive, beneficial, happy imaginings are challenged and God and the Devil have their playground on earth.

But we have free will and we can create through imagining conditions that are beneficial. In fact, that is the reason we come back; to lessen that karma and work towards grace and play a more constructive role for ourselves and all concerned. And I think that is exactly why we're here. To imagine beauty when history tells us life or the world is ugly.

- - -

Imagining is at its best when it isn't a completely cerebral act. It is best accompanied by a unified heart. A solid sense of how we would like it, ourselves, and it all to be. A commitment to your heart's desire. Never allow your ego and your mind's hunger for center stage intimidate what your heart and gut tell you. It's helpful to develop this and be freed of trying to orchestrate results. If you can cultivate a unified heart in harmony with your imagining, then there is really no figuring you need to do.

There's really no acting or way of acting or particular course of action that is required. To do so is like treating the symptom. Working at changing acts is working backwards.

The acts, the sense, the logic, will follow as a result of winning the challenge of the imagination.

- - -

OK. Now let's go one step further. It's clear that we can't just go around imagining whatever we want and it will all come true. We share this world with many other beings who also have the power of imagining. So let's say I can imagine peace but someone else can imagine war. All of what I've already said is still true but as a community, as a unit, as parts of a whole, it hangs in the balance of our individual imaginings.

My imaginings can't make anybody else do or believe anything or make them want me or make them decide anything favorable towards me. But my imaginings makes me a vital participant and a responsible creator as does everyone else's.

It might seem at first that someone selfish, greedy, or power hungry would simply choose dominance and have it free of retribution, but that's not the case. In group and community dynamics there are combinations of imagining. There are infinite gradations of both imaginings with little impact on other beings and imaginings with great impact on other beings. If one person's imaginings impact another's comfort and "well-being" then there is conflict. With free will and the complexity of our desires it can get messy. That's where commonality comes in. If groups of beings having similar ideals and desires can combine their wills and imaginings, they will have more influence. One can only hope that the desire we all have for the health of the world is greater than the desire for dominance over others.

- - -

And we, us humans, are not alone here. I believe that accepting or assuming that all things, the rocks, the weather, the planets are all a part of a greater whole, they would all share the power of imagining. And it would explain the relationships of all things and their unique vibrations contributing in their unique ways to our combined imagining and the consequent creating of the world and the universe as we know it.

We, as more conscious beings, however, having a greater power of imagination, with a long reach, therefore carry more responsibility to use our free will to achieve harmony. We need to recognize and honor the (s)lower beings who are "happy" with less demands in space and time. Rocks aren't that picky. There is much flexibility in imagining relationships with a rock without it dynamically affecting the community.

Also there are slower vibrating beings - trees for example – who may not extend as far in their imagining as other beings individually, but a forest or planetary community of trees and their unity with weather, water, etc. does compel a level of natural law to be reckoned with.

\- - -

I'll finish this theme with some thoughts on the power of imagining over history and sequential life.

\- - -

We must recognize and believe that our history isn't our fate. It's simply that there are times when our guard is down and we lose the faith and imagine the worst or at least imagine less than we desire. Be certain of this; our history isn't proof of any pattern beyond our completely self fulfilling prophesy.

From my journals:

> During my run that I just got back from I was thinking about the traps of sequential acts. It occurred to me that there are physical limitations. Like I'm in the same body that historically took a couple of months to develop solid running shape. Then I decided to change that to physical "predispositions." As a spirit we have chosen our body, our astrology, our others to gather together with, and we have made our contracts with ourselves. But all of this is only our predisposition. We are free agents. We decide ultimately what choices we will make, regardless of the volume and intensity of the committee voices; each with their own agenda.
>
> Tonight I feel like I'm mustering my courage to blow my life apart. I mean to blow apart the linear conservative sequence, safely chosen to accommodate patterns of behavior that appear falsely to be wisdom. And to shed society's idea of

sanity; a safe sequential predictable course. Normal and utterly perverse.

- - -

I have noticed that whenever I move or I'm in a new place where people don't know me that I have an opportunity to kind of start over. I don't feel as timid to do nutty things that normally make me feel self conscious. Once I feel people know me, I get the feeling that it's harder to act differently. I feel the energy of their thinking, "wow, this is out of character." There is a word in German, Narrenfreiheit, which means fool's freedom. Yeah. The fool's freedom that we all should have. And not just to feel nutty, but much more importantly to break the threads of limitations and to break out of our little boxes.

- - -

In conversation with a friend of a roommate, he expressed his distaste for people asking what he did, meaning work, etc. I said make up tales. Spin a fanciful yarn. Cloak it all and have fun. The truth is that anyone worth their salt would know more about you from your foolishness and spontaneous creativity than from any list of life facts.

- - -

I once saw a movie that was a beautiful example of the power of overcoming the hold of sequential life. It was called "Another Woman" with Justine Bateman. She had lost her memory. She finds herself in a relationship with a loving caring man (her husband) who doesn't trust her. They essentially start over, she being now sweet and loving, the sequence of her behavior in her crumbling marriage broken. She and her husband slowly rebuild trust and loving before she discovers the blame and unforgiving that had put distance between them the first time around; she now ready to let it go.

--- 

Yes, imagine yourself how and who you would like to be. Use your unified heart in concert with your imaginings. Try and not be limited by your sequential life and your history. When you are imagining, shuck all limitations. Imagine your dreams coming true. Remember, you can't and shouldn't try to override someone else's free will to engage in their own personal imagining. You can't have everything you want just by imagining, but you can shape yourself and your interactions for the most positive and highest quality possibilities.

# Sensing, Feeling, Thinking

Be aware when engaging the mind. The mind is a great tool, but you should proceed with caution when it makes your decisions or dominates your behavior; particularly when communicating with others. Featuring logic or psychological thinking can severely hamper communications skills. The natural flow and timing can easily be overridden.

Live in your body.

Living in your head is not good. The head is meant to be visited. Unlike the body, there is no indoor plumbing to eliminate waste. When the mind is only visited it remains uncluttered so that fresh, creative, innovative thinking can be put to use. Sensory input is allowed to come in unmolested and will pass through beautifully. Old baggage, repeated thoughts, and old tape loops create dross and clog things up and will eventually seep into the body.

I'm sure there are people who believe that to live in the body is heathen and hedonistic; that the head is where intellect, logic, philosophy, belief, and values are to be found.

Yes, it is true that the reflective mind has its role, but all of those aspects of the mind are easily corrupted, hypnotized, co-opted and perverted. The qualities of truth and goodness and health and righteousness are things you feel in your heart, in your gut. And in your muscles.

The head predominant is insufficient and reckless at best, dangerous at worst.

- - -

There are those who believe that in order to get it all together and to seek to be part of the whole, the best way is to escape this plane and the physical. I call this cosmic escapism.

The irony is that the fastest way to get out of your body attachment is to get into your body. It is the body that holds us here and there is a reason for that. It's kind of like an apprenticeship. You have to learn to manage and run a body before you can move on.

- - -

There is a lot of misunderstanding about what I call inharmonious acts of passion, better know as bad deeds. People get into their head and when it directs and orchestrates all of the body's dramas, they think they're into their body. Then they think the body is the culprit. The body gets blamed. This is a shame.

This has resulted in a lot of puritanical attitudes that continue to screw up just about every culture on earth.

The body and emotions get a bad name because of the misunderstanding of how the process of denial and the mind's dis-ease compel inharmonious acts of passion. Inharmonious acts of passion are determined by a psychology, which is a (subconscious) mental choice to be selective as to what's believed from what's taken in from parent, bible, teachers, and the scientist.

Where does psychology come from, which is to say why do we selectively believe what we are "taught" or selectively believe what we experience? From needs not met. From holes needing to be filled and from the radar that screens out what is too challenging.

Why is it too challenging? Because we have limited our feelings and consequently our experiences and have fear of the unknown. Experience means allowing our surroundings and senses to affect us. That means really fully experiencing, not just "doing" something new that is physically new but that can be packaged neatly within certain parameters.

So it is the limiting of feelings and the limiting of sensing information and not the indulgence in them that starts the chain reaction that leads the mind to direct distorted acts.

---

While talking with a friend he said that one would hope that leaders would want to promote unity or something like that. I said to him that I believed that the reason that so many of our leaders are involved in politics and law is because they fear natural flow and need to support control and constraints.

He said he hoped the fear wouldn't bring them down to the animal level. Fact of the matter is, as I see it, that a person acting on fear and adding human ingenuity to it, extends below the animal level. I kind of see this picture of a pivot point of animal naiveté. With pureness of action (however much or lack thereof) and our intent tipping us above or below that level. It is not the physical animal that we are that is responsible but the intent that drives it. And that intent is vulnerable as a function of the mind. The body and the senses don't lie. They simply cannot. It is the head's interpretation that distorts the input.

---

I have always been very sensitive to noise, garish visual assaults, awful and toxic smells and so on. Many people have said to me, don't worry, you'll get used to it. I think it is a function of the mind to stop awareness of the body's messages if a choice has been made to continue to co-exist with some undesirable influence. It is a kind of survival mechanism. But it is also a trap. It is sometimes hard to realize that you've stopped sensing or feeling something because of a "good reason" but now that reason has passed. So you continue being numb.

What a cheat of our senses and body information.

Similarly, I have noticed that sometimes when I experience something and I am not satisfied with what I feel, I will seek to control the situation by explaining it. Once I've explained it, that can tend to limit the sensory and feeling input. The mind's reasoning based on sensory and feeling input must be fluid. Labeling and attaching finality to something can close the book on it, when there is, for sure, so much more of the story to be told.

- - -

Society teaches us to use speech to share experience. It also attempts to teach us to inhibit the body and emotions so as to not "reflect" experience. But the body must and will, as a creature of nature, reflect experience. Speech becomes a substitute used all too often as a contrived tool dedicated to communicating experience in common or traditional terms; a safer way to convey and share experience than allowing the body to express itself naturally and fully.

Children use their bodies freely to express themselves. If they are upset they might, for example, stomp their feet, tilt their head and scrunch up their face. We, society, as adults, feel it is out of line to make a scene. We fall back on words. This is not only unfortunate because we fail to communicate fully but also because in the process we lose the ability to truly read what another is communicating to us. Certainly we all read body language to some extent, but it is severely limited.

Also, anytime we choose to inhibit the body's reflecting of our inner feelings, there is a physical price to pay. If the body's natural response is not allowed full expression, it will be manifested as tension or stress somewhere within the body.

- - -

Emotions function as signals. If you hold on to any emotion because of a mental attachment or for ulterior motives, then there may not be a place for another emotion to surface to show your true response to new thoughts or conditions. Try to not crystallize, categorize, or package your emotions. This will allow new unobstructed emotions to surface and be fully experienced and then yield to new ones.

This exception, from my journals:

> When I was questioning the role of emotions and suggesting they could pass after having shown us what prompted them, I wondered about love and contented emotion and sustaining beautiful desirable emotions. Right now I feel that by learning from and respecting the lessons of the emotions that arise, they will pass, however it could be possible to maintain an underlying contented non-dramatic love. And the way I feel right now, I would also say my love is not directed. People that shine in my presence are recognized warmly but it's not because of or for them I feel this love. I believe that there is a kind of pure love that could be sustained

without needing to yield in order to allow the free flow of new emotions.

- - -

And the following is a journal entry from a time when I was living in Santa Cruz, a California beach town, that offers some thought regarding the power of the mind over the body and how it can get "hung up" rather than letting go and allowing something to pass:

Today I drove by the market across the street from Teva's at 41st and Portola and remembered the time I was in there and a woman was in there wearing a small bikini and how much it excited me, especially being away from the beach.

I found it very curious and revelatory to realize that if I had seen her yesterday, dressed in the same bikini, when I was at the hot springs where everybody was naked, it probably wouldn't have left such an impression. And yet, although I'm in a different state now, the original charge and impulse are still there. "Impression" is a good word for it. It's not even "me" now but I still feel, with this memory, the titillation and uneasiness and the feelings of yearning and incompleteness. I feel it now, even as I write, in my nerves, in my arms. Quite amazing how a mere memory, having no reality in the present can continue to generate its original impulse. And it seems that it takes more spiritual work and conviction and knowing to pacify that charge imprinted in my body, than it does a similar event in physical reality in the present. It seems to me that this theme deserves attention. Maybe I need to reword, re-edit the memory. Not the memory, actually. I think it is good to allow it to be, but to disengage the tendrils still wrapped around my nervous system.

It's like how sometimes when in a state of grace you can still observe the flotsam and jetsam of your past trials and tribulations without being affected by them. I think it would be healthy to use those times to address past entanglements and to try and allow them and their charge to pass.

- - -

I have given some thought to the three possible orders in which people think, feel, and act. For each individual there must be many variables depending on circumstances and on one's past history in similar situations. People probably have predominate patterns but vary them with conditions and how secure they are, and other factors. For example, faced with a critical choice, thinking first would often be wise. Under attack I might act first. With a lover under soft lights I might feel first, let that guide my actions, and minimize and put thinking on a back burner.

I think we could all learn a lot about ourselves by observing the order in which we think, feel and act.

- - -

In conclusion let me say this. The dynamics of sensing, feeling, and thinking is truly mind boggling. Which is exactly why we should live in the body. Somewhere under our confusions, the body is telling us the truth.

# Reminders

## Reminders Preface

When I reread my journals in order to log them and make them accessible I organized a group of entries that were meant as reminders to myself. From time to time I look at these and find myself reminded of things that I had seen so clearly at one particular moment, in one environment, and among certain circumstances in the flow of my life, and am often surprised; yeah, I knew that then.

Some of these reminders, whether regarding actions or attitudes, arose from contemplation and some from times I caught myself engaging in or featuring them and noticed the therapeutic benefit. I say therapeutic, but it is so much more than that. Many of these reminders are attitudes which clean house and give more space for the new and for necessary change.

It is so easy to forget and be swept along. Sometimes by events. Sometimes by the attitudes and agendas of other people we come into contact with. Sometimes by people we never meet but who seem to influence our society and make demands on our lives. But perhaps, mostly, by the pressures we put on ourselves relative to all the external things of one's life.

It will be noted by the shrewd reader that some of these reminders may seem to contradict each other. No doubt there is some truth to that. But each serves, I believe, to stimulate awareness of various aspects of life and various times and places along our paths. I leave them to be considered and applied when they seem helpful.

Many of these reminders mean something to me in the context of my life by just reading the one line title, but in putting this collection together I have expanded on each one a little. In the process of assembling these reminders, I find myself affected; finding myself more reflective. They seem to be having the effect that was the whole point of organizing this group of journal entries in the first place.

My hope is that they can be of some value to others as well.

# Reminders Contents

**Reminders**..................................................94

Decide to be Positive....................................94
Pay Attention to Messages From the Universe........95
Recognize the Issues and Dramas of Your Life
    as Part of Your Own Particular Style................96
Seek to be in the Center of Your Life........................97
Soak Up the Good That Comes Your Way
    and Let the Unpleasant Slip By........................98
Singing Out Loud is of Tremendous Benefit
    to the Soul..........................................................98
Choose Times of Music and Sound Receptivity;
    Not Louding Upon the World...........................99
Say Hello to People as Spirits.....................................99
Love Everyone Always Because… Who Knows?..100
Stay in Time, Allow Time's Natural Continuity.......101
Be a Human Being, Not a Human Doing...............102
Don't be Attached to Previous Successes
    (or Failures).......................................................103
Live in Your Body, Not in Your Head.......................104
Recognize That Your Body is its Own Animal,
    You are its Steward..........................................105
Don't Hide From or Suppress the Undesirable,
    Allow the Uncalculating Primitive..................105
Do What Gives You Power in the Bigger Picture..106
Stay Aware of What Your Own Energy Is...............107

Release Others to Their Greater Good...................108
Focus on the Strengthening of Yourself
    and Your Own Ideals.........................................109
Seek the Sources of Problems but Recognize
    That Things Springing From the Source Can
    Take on a Life of Their Own............................110
Never Hate Yourself...................................................111
Avoid Adding Fire to Issues Being Discussed,
    Allow Others to Save Face...............................112
If You Feel the Need to be in Control,
    Try Instead to be in Awareness.......................113
The Oversight Principle.............................................114
Delight in Truth at all Costs......................................115
Don't Get Caught in the Looking for Results Trap 116
Adopt a Child's View of Life.....................................117
Check it Out: Does This Bring me Pleasure?........118
Aesthetics and Values Will Carry You
    When Knowing Can't........................................120

# Shorty Reminders...........................121
# One Liner Reminders..................124

# Reminders

## Decide to be Positive

Deciding to be positive is no small thing. I made a decision at one point in my life to turn over a new leaf; to decide to be positive. At that time many subtle things combined to make me feel like changing myself. I decided to profoundly change my vibration and thoroughly change my attitude and my daily behavior and responses to the events of the day. Much of it was of a spiritual nature; the awareness of something grander than the struggles of what non-dreamers like to refer to as "reality." So I just decided to glow; to vibrate at a higher vibration. I touched more. And I smiled a lot.

Almost immediately people seemed to respond to me differently. Without going into details, suffice to say that the world opened up to me in the weeks following that decision.

Now this arose organically from my life at that time but that does not mean that its lesson is any less valid or that it is not possible to manifest such a change by willing it at any time. There is always some "reality" that will pose a challenge if we decide to vibrate at a higher level, but we have the power of choice. Believing fully in this positive outlook and behavior is helpful, but short of that, to just act it and keep pushing yourself to outwardly express it can also yield results. Make yourself over in spirit.

Know that you are making it happen for yourself. Be forward and bold beautifully. When engaging with others, any words will do if you glow enough… and smile.

## Pay Attention to Messages From the Universe

Think about dreams. Dreams are a symbolic play. Each character, each prop, and each act tell you something about yourself. They are symbolic, I believe, so that you have to participate in the sleuthing to unravel the mysteries of your own life. And as such they are an offered opportunity.

If you think about it life is full of such opportunities; messages that come in many forms and give us signs and information. When I first had the epiphany that made me aware of this as such a powerful tool I couldn't help but feel like I'd been a fool for not taking advantage of them. And that expression is really the key: take advantage of them.

But short of taking advantage of them, the first step is just to even recognize them and stop and say – woah, there is an opportunity. Even if you choose not to act on it, know it was offered and was there; something was offered to you and could be a tool to help you gain insight.

I made a list of where such messages might come from. By no means is this a complete list (I doubt there is such an animal) but a good starter.

- Dreams
- Bio-feedback – the body's response to things (everything and always, really)
- Emotional feedback – emotional response to things (everything and always)

- Chance meetings – encountering people
- Chance happenings – events or situations encountered
- Chance shared information – from any source - in person, TV, radio, book, computer
- Chance overhearings - something overheard in passing on the street or somebody talking in a restaurant or cafe, for example

Stay alert to messages from all quarters and make your own list.

## Recognize the Issues and Dramas of Your Life as Part of Your Own Particular Style

If you can accept the nature of progressing through life's days as your own style, it can help to bring the responsibility for your actions home. Responsibility sounds heavy and maybe burdensome, but with accepting that it is your own style comes also the opportunity to apply your own unique approach to the possibilities of dealing with whatever you need to. It's your game. Try and make the rules work for you. And maybe, above all, don't let others define your approach to dealing with things. It is, after all, your life.

Advice from others is ok. Listening is good. But don't accept others' advice and solutions straight out. Try them on, see how they fit. And tailor them to your style.

It's your life. Validate and empower your style, your approach, your solutions.

## Seek to be in the Center of Your Life

Be in the here and now. You've heard it said a thousand times. But more than that, be in the center of your life. Be inside your life. More than just taking part in life, you are the place it all comes from. The source.

Imagine the despair of someone not consciously participating in life. Just being done to. Instead, validate your life and the creativity of your choices. It's you. Live life like the game is afoot. In high school I ran cross country and before the race began I'd be all nervous and out-of-sorts. I'd feel tight and awkward until the starting gun went off, then I was suddenly free - I was doing it. It was up to me. Working things out thrills me; wondering what will happen irks me and drags me.

Be on a mission.

Be in the center of your life; in time and in space. Be hungry but be careful that your longing for something doesn't lead you away from the center of your life to somewhere or something you hope or expect to be.

Don't wait for the "whens" and the "if onlys", thinking or believing that once something happens, then you'll whatever. Contribute to life somehow; your life, all life. If life isn't flowing, develop a course of action, do the best you can, trust nature, carry on. If you need time out to emote, grieve, or feel it to give up, allow yourself that; but temporarily.

## Soak Up the Good That Comes Your Way and Let the Unpleasant Slip By

There was a time when I was very aware of myself struggling with unpleasant feelings. And I remembered an old philosophy of mine. And that was that as I passed through time and space, to absorb and go with the good coming my way and to let the bad slide by. I would feature an image of myself standing straight and broad when I encountered something good and desirable so as to take it in and absorb it and feel it fully and when I encountered something unpleasant I would turn a side to it and make myself narrow, making it easier for it to slip by.

## Singing Out Loud is of Tremendous Benefit to the Soul

This is not earth shaking news, but, I believe, a simple truth. Singing out loud is of tremendous benefit to the soul. Do it often. It works on so many levels. It can be a distraction from worry. Or perhaps it's a better use of words to think of it as a replacement for worry. I don't think it's healthy to deny and suppress issues but incessant worry eats away at body and soul, and singing out loud can take you to a different place. Also there is the actual resonance. There is healing in sound and vibration.

## Choose Times of Music and Sound Receptivity; Not Louding Upon the World

Another reminder suggested singing out loud. So now I suggest not singing out loud. Go figure. There is a time and place for everything. I had an experience once when I was singing along with some music when I had a touch of laryngitis and it was uncomfortable so I decided to just listen. I became aware that the music became more crystalline as I changed my energy to receptiveness. And, continuing on through the day as I consciously chose to be quiet and still my larynx, I became aware of acoustics and much of the subtle nature of my surroundings. To be quiet consciously is not just quiet non-speaking moments, but an attitude of not projecting, not louding upon the world. An attitude of receptiveness.

And applied in another way, I was with a friend of mine who is a real talker (enjoyably so) and instead of responding and pitching in and head tripping on and on with him, I just nodded my head and took it in. My awareness of him and his message; his style; the unique life that he has came clearer to me. Occasional larynx-free days or periods of time can really enhance appreciation.

## Say Hello to People as Spirits

I must admit that I don't say hello to people as spirits enough. I do, in some moods, in some spaces, but all too often I'm engulfed in the physical; reacting to their acting. Or perhaps trying to understand their psychology behind their behavior.

These ways of thinking about and viewing others is often a reaction to wanting to understand why things aren't as we feel they should be; whether it's somebody we are close to or a stranger on the street or even a part of our society that is disturbing to us. This has the effect of making us in some way demanding.

See people as spirits. Free them to their potential. That sounds quite altruistic, as there are certainly many individuals whose actions seem destructive or obtrusive. But, truth is, it only clutters their space and muddles their ability to grow when we reduce someone to being nothing more than their acts and their personality. Disagreement is fine. It's part of living socially. But remain aware of the role they play as spirits on the same stage we all share.

This sounds like it is all about making nice for the sake of others, but seeing others as spirits helps remind us that we ourselves are spirits and helps us stay on the high road.

## Love Everyone Always Because… Who Knows?

Loving everyone in an altruistic way is certainly a good practice. But in terms of everyday encounters with other humans we meet, there are some nuts and bolts things that need to be considered. Certainly we have and need to make choices regarding what vibrations we exist among and with whom we intimately co-mingle. And it is natural to want to be selective and check people out for fit first, before you invest much energy.

There have been times when I was so tired of loss and disappointment that I wanted to completely withdraw from the game. I retreated, believing that whoever is right for me I'll be certain about from the start. And I didn't want to deal with the complexities of the getting to know each other's trepidations. Or I was afraid of the disappointment.

But this really does take you out of the game. Not only do you have blinders on, but the walls are perceived by others. We really do need to take chances on hidden loving behind not so obvious faces if we expect that in return from the universe.

So, the bottom line is this. Appreciate people for what they have to offer; not just how they are now to you. You don't have to jump into relating to anyone but see them at face value, allow them to be, allow yourself to see them as dynamic and vital with qualities and capabilities and not just how they fit you right at that moment.

So much for nuts and bolts. Complete the circle. Back to loving everyone always because.... who knows? It really is the high road. It is such a simple truth. Feel the love within. Don't think in terms of wanting anyone to be different or trying to change someone's mind. Instead, behave in such a way that you reach their hearts instead.

That should be enough for its own sake.

Also, maybe you are off your game and not seeing deeply enough. Maybe someone will surprise you and turn out to be someone you will value having in your life. Who knows?

## Stay in Time, Allow Time's Natural Continuity

There was a week when I wanted time to go by fast; I was looking forward to something and was being impatient. And then when that week of waiting and being distracted by my impatience was over I wished I had gotten more done.

There were a few things that really needed doing that I hadn't gotten done. What a fool I had been, thinking I could mess with time. It's always going to win.

Try to feel or maybe realize a sense of continuity in the events of your life. Be aware of the thread in the attitudes you hold regarding those events. Paradoxically, try to not try. Just allow it. Also paradoxically, taking time, not rushing, is the best way to get the most out of the precious time each of us has. Rhythm.

## Be a Human Being, Not a Human Doing

Doing is a fine thing. It is essential to life. But is life defined by our doing? I don't think so. That's too much of a burden to carry; to define ourselves by our doing. Don't get in the way of your essential purity. Don't push yourself into a model or characterize yourself by your doing.

Put another way, it's important to keep separate, in mind and attitude, life itself from the stuff of life. I once wrote in my journal, "I feel too stuck in my life to be me. 'My life' has become bigger than me." I had been looking at footage of Gene Kelly dancing and of a woman rock climbing and was feeling hurt and feeling self pity for all that I haven't done and never will do. This is, of course, a very human mood. But it is me judging myself by my doing. Not the being of my heart and soul.

Treat your life as an independent force.

## Don't be Attached to Previous Successes (or Failures)

It's natural to want to repeat previous successes. It feels good to accomplish something of value and who can blame you for wanting to repeat that success. But life just doesn't work that way. The environment will always have changed in some way. Certainly, it's fine to apply the same skills or gifts in other ventures. But the energy and the act of the past is gone.

Once when I was replaying some event from my past and trying to get off on it, I felt how it wasn't clean; wasn't right. It came to me that past events are helpful when brought up to teach, show, give perspective to other events and to learn from about the linkages in one's own life. But to revel in them or try and relive them is a waste of time and energy. I came back to the present and felt more whole.

It's a subtle thing but there needs to be a certain level of non-attachment to free you to the same power you had in creating a successful experience in the first place. Feeling free of history and believing in what is flowing to and by and all around you gives you the clean slate to work on.

Using sports as an analogy, if you gloat and focus on the one great play you've just made, you'll miss the next opportunity. You've got to get back in the present and be enthused with what's facing you now. Playing music literally and in life metaphorically, you've got to let one note go to hear the next.

Likewise, feeling or believing that past failures or the time that has passed since peak moments indicates your life, is not true - quite the contrary; more likely they bind you to the old and used up. Interesting concept - we try and repeat the old successes and fret and struggle against past failures or losses, but hey!, they're used now. They're history. And who wants a used experience?

## Live in Your Body, Not in Your Head

Be aware when engaging the mind. The mind is a great tool, but you should proceed with caution when it makes your decisions or dominates your behavior; particularly when communicating with others. Featuring logic or psychological thinking can severely hamper communications skills. The natural flow and timing can easily be overridden.

The head is meant to be visited. Unlike the body, there is no indoor plumbing to eliminate waste. When the mind is only visited it remains uncluttered so that fresh, creative, innovative thinking can be put to use. Sensory input is allowed to come in unmolested and will pass through beautifully. Old baggage, repeated thoughts, and old tape loops create dross and clog things up. And will eventually seep into the body.

It is true that the reflective mind has its role, but intellect, logic, philosophy, belief, and even values are easily corrupted, hypnotized, co-opted and perverted. The qualities of truth and goodness and health and righteousness are things you feel in your heart, in your gut. And in your muscles.

Live in your body; where truth is truth.

## Recognize That Your Body is its Own Animal, You are its Steward

One night, lying in bed I had a powerful, clear, unique personal experience. I thought about my body and suddenly got this deep rush of compassion for my body and realized in that moment and glow that it's just ego to think that it's my slave; "my" body to do with as I choose. It is its own animal. As we are stewards of the earth, so are we stewards of our bodies. I felt shocked how I've assumed my dominion over it. I felt that I owed it many apologies. And I begged its understanding for my bumbling.

A corollary to this would be to realize that the body's natural state is to exist in radiant health. And that most of the pain and shortcomings and dis-eases of the body come from our mismanagement of it. Whether it be from foisting upon it, internally or externally, that which it has no use for and that which is toxic to it or whether it be from the stress we subject it to by our attitudes and anxieties.

Seek a harmonious relationship, recognizing the body's sovereignty and intelligence.

## Don't Hide From or Suppress the Undesirable, Allow the Uncalculating Primitive

Once, when feeling completely incapable of effecting change in myself or in creating conditions in my life that would help bring change about, I wrote the following:

"I pollute my body with 'food' and constipate my system with a mental life that is addicted to the attachment to a personality that runs from shadow to shadow, forever eluding the golden light of my real self."

Be bold and aggressive and unafraid. You need not protect yourself from rejection or hurt or especially the loss of whichever face it is you feel you need to retain. You are a piece of art in the making. Believe that in any arena you can find a way. In a way it's a call to the primitive in us. Allow the uncalculating primitive. Do what needs to be done without being so calculating. To be sure, be careful to temper this freedom we all have with the creed of non-violence but flee the shadows and deal with whatever the light exposes. It is really the only way to tap the awesome personal power that is your birthright.

## Do What Gives You Power in the Bigger Picture

If you look around and observe what people do, both unassuming acts and acts that are done as a statement of some sort, you may wonder why they choose to express themselves in such a manner. They are doing it because on some level they think it is effective.

We do things because we think it gives us power. Essentially that's what we all do, to some extent all the time; everything we do, every act. We do what we think gives us our power, brings us our power, leads us to our power.

Why then do we seem to waste our power or choose paths of denial and avoidance of positive responsible behavior.

That's the trap. We might waste time or act out physically in ways that fall short of our ideals or seem to exhibit a lack of introspection, but that is us choosing the shortsightedness of the avoidance of the pain or the discomfort of acts that challenge our status quo. Avoiding a challenge and the struggle to overcome the way we are can seem to give us more power than the outcome of the struggle would ultimately give us.

And perhaps the challenge in all growth and spiritual unfoldment is to recognize that the result of taking on challenges and breaking through will lead to a kind of harmony and flow and trust and faith that really does increase our power. Try and see the bigger picture.

## Stay Aware of What Your Own Energy Is

Do your best to be in your body and to be free of others' energy.

First, learn to be fully present in your own body and endeavor to stay in your own body. Take stock of yourself from head to toe. Try to not be "spaced out" or distracted. Tip the balance of what occupies your mind towards an awareness of your senses and your physical surroundings rather than the thoughts in your head.

Endeavor to know yourself. Just think, if you really knew yourself; really knew what is you and your creations for your life and your body, how effective you could be, both for yourself and others. The viewpoint would be so clear. It's like when hiking through the wild, how sometimes you need to find a high place to reconnoiter to help you decide what you best do or in what direction you best go.

Secondly, try and be aware of what is your own energy and what you may be picking up from those around you and the people closest to you in your life. The more you are in touch with your own body and in the present, the easier it is to recognize the energy that isn't your own.

It is completely natural to take on the energy of other people with whom we are in contact. This is part of communicating. But if you are not aware of or lose awareness of what energy is yours and what is theirs, it can be disconcerting and unhealthy. It is confusing to feel someone else's pains, physical or emotional; their created reality.

Think about how we all have our own unique chosen realities; our bodies, pains, parents, astrology and histories. Just imagine what a shock it would be to trade bodies with someone else. To suddenly deal with someone else's stuff would be pretty demanding and probably not very comfortable. If you take on someone else's energy, you don't have the context to deal with it.

I feel like I should mention here that being consolidated in your own body does not, in fact, isolate you in the sense that you are not or cannot be one with others in a spiritual sense or human sense. In fact it is actually a paradox that the better you know your self, the more easily and effectively you can participate with all. And when you are not taking on the drama that someone else is involved in, you are in a better position to help that person, should you choose to.

## Release Others to Their Greater Good

Releasing others to their greater good is a powerful tool.

To hold someone in contempt is a selfish act. And destructive for all parties involved. By doing so the other person is constantly carrying your bad vibes and you are contributing to any difficulty they may have achieving and moving towards their greatest good. Make a bit of a ritual about it. Don't just think it; really release them to their own unfettered unfoldment.

If you feel anger or disappointment towards anyone, first love yourself for feeling that way and look for the truth that by loving yourself and not feeling bad about it, you free yourself to your goodness. Then release them. It may not solve all the issues, but it lightens the load for everyone.

## Focus on the Strengthening of Yourself and Your Own Ideals

The need for recognition seems to be a fundamental human quality. I believe, however, that ultimately, as an individual, as a participant in this great experiment on this planet, it is important to seek a place within where you have very little need for recognition.

What's important is to validate yourself for simply being who you are and what you give and not to care about what you get back. The thing is to participate and share what you do and how you feel without feeling that your center (your self) is compromised. And don't judge what you're giving by what others are receiving or what you are by what others are perceiving. Ultimately you have no control over that.

Also when confronted with the ugly or undesirable, try and not fight against it. Rather, focus on the strengthening of yourself and your own ideals. We function better in life when we are flexible. Flexibility is easier when it's not indicative of, or seen as, a compromise of self; easier when you're not changing because you think you ought to or you need to, in order to fit something or someone else's ideas or ideals.

## Seek the Sources of Problems but Recognize That Things Springing From the Source Can Take on a Life of Their Own

In an interview I once heard somebody say: Drugs are not the source of the problem, but they take on a life of their own. This concept could be applied to many habits, relationship patterns, arguments, and socially indoctrinated living styles. Even the machines and mechanics of our lifestyle choices.

Like if you are depressed about something so you feel like just sitting around instead of taking your daily walk. The indolence and the lack of exercise are consequences of the way you deal with the depression, but they take on a life of their own. Inertia has a way of growing and the longer you go without exercise, the less you feel like doing it.

So if you catch yourself in any kind of destructive behavior, seek the cause or root of it; ultimately identifying the source is important. But, having taken on a life of its own, working on overcoming bad habits or responses to the original issue also has merit. It keeps the situation from being compounded and it helps remove obstacles to identifying and dealing with the source issue.

One very practical example is stress. Stress itself is unhealthy in many ways. And it's easy to say you are stressed because you have so much to do or because of this or that. But think – is that really the source of the stress? Often the answer is no; that itself isn't inherently stress producing. The event that seem to be the cause of the stress isn't usually the source of the stress, but the stress has taken on a life of its own. Work on mollifying the stress in order to circle back and find its roots.

## Never Hate Yourself

After having been in a phase of feeling really in tune, I noticed how as my rhythm failed I got down on myself. I began saying negative things about myself. It really struck me deeply as I became aware of it.

It really struck me that you should just never put yourself self down. But how do you deal with being disappointed in yourself or observing yourself making choices that you are critical of?

I would say try try try to love anything you can. Yourself if you can. If you can't, someone else maybe. If you can't, the weather maybe. Or how you were. A choice you once made. A time you helped someone. Or even a time you accepted help. Anything.

You have a right to be here and there are no requirements. Your existence alone is valuable. Just don't hate yourself. The consequences and implications are so extensive.

So, let me say this:

Never, ever, under any circumstance, for any reason, no matter what, under any conditions, ever, regardless, absolutely, ever, at anytime, anywhere, with or because of anybody or any event, ever dislike yourself.    Got it??!!!

## Avoid Adding Fire to Issues Being Discussed, Allow Others to Save Face

Suppressing issues out of fear of the conflict is unhealthy and makes most situations just get worse. Bring things up without being in conflict mode. Don't assume an issue will be a conflict. As a participant, we have a lot of power to defuse potentially hot issues.

It's often the case that the problem is more in the consequences of avoiding bringing things up than in the original issue. Many apparent disagreements are not irreconcilable and turn out to be just social blunders and not really problems as such. Look for opportunities to laugh together at the misunderstandings. Sometimes two people just have different ideas about the implications of a certain act and when it's understood what it means to each of them, it's not that hard to find a middle ground.

Avoid adding fire to conversations by not correcting people if they measure you incorrectly. Avoid giving your opinion when it adds fire to a critical conversation just because you feel a need to defend yourself or your position. Feeling like you have to defend yourself only creates an us vs. them tenor to the discussion.

And one of the most powerful tools in conflict resolution is to allow others to save face. Sometimes, especially when some issue has grown over time, people will really begin to own a certain stance. Seeking a way to resolve the issue while not openly calling the other person out for their stance helps a lot to soften the middle ground.

Quietly, within yourself, forgive the other person (and yourself) without insisting on an apology, regardless of your actual appraisal of the sources of the issue. Realize that you possess a power that no one else can take away from you.

## If You Feel the Need to be in Control, Try Instead to be in Awareness

When feeling like life is running you around, it is easy to have a sense of futility or despair. You feel out of control, vulnerable to influences that are taking you places you don't really want to go. This is bound to happen at times. Most likely it has to do with lack of flexibility. I don't mean the that your lack of flexibility is causing the events or forces that are taking you for a ride, but rather your flexibility determines how bumpy the ride is.

There are ways and techniques that a person can employ to have more control; visualization, imagination, trying to orchestrate or perhaps choreograph the events. (Or, of course, you could try and push back against the forces with your own force – good luck on that one.)

But the fact of the matter is, you really can't control in totality all of what is going on around and with you. Although we all possess a certain amount of power and we all play our own parts in directing events, there are just too many other people and other external forces at play.

So, when you feel the need to be in control, try instead to be in awareness. In awareness you can best function utilizing yourself during any experience. Although you have free will, so do others around you so there are no guarantees. But… the more aware you are of the physical forces at play and the vibrations and intentions of the people at play, the better equipped you are to find a comfortable groove.

And the more your awareness increases, the higher your vibration will be, which allows you to kind of buzz around within the chaos of the world and find the spaces amidst its juggernaut.

## The Oversight Principle

In a conversation with a friend of mine he said he wanted to stop stumbling along, just trying to make spiritual sense out of events as they occurred. He wanted to stop just acting out of habit and was inspired by some Rudolph Steiner he had been reading to apply himself more scientifically towards spiritual goals; to make conscious choices.

That reminded me of two lessons in my life.

The first was when I was with two others, one of who was looking all over for something they had lost; looking kind of haphazardly and undirected. The other man, named Don Overstreet was someone I knew to be pretty analytical; more so than appeals to me. But he said something to the man who was floundering in his search that has stuck with me. He said, Stop. Right where you are. Look around. Take stock of the situation. Think. Proceed rationally.

That so impressed me that I have, employing a word play, named it The Oversight Principle, oversight having two quite different meanings. It can mean to fail to see something. But it also means to watch over or tend something.

Far beyond just trying to find something, the Oversight Principle can be employed in many arenas of life. One such case would be when a physical ailment appears. Instead of simply ruing the discomfort or impairment, seek whence it came. Stop and ask yourself when it was that you first noticed it, are there other related symptoms or feelings, how were you feeling emotionally then and now. Or when you find yourself reacting to a situation, stop and take a moment to track the situation. What led to this situation, what actions or events brought you to this point. In the case of an issue with a person, take a breath and look at the thread in the events or perhaps in a conversation and try and get a clear idea of the bigger picture. Use the Oversight Principle also when reflecting on things in general. There is inevitably a series of events or thoughts or something that offers insight into where you now are.

The second lesson I was reminded of is the story of the person who is dedicated to progressing and achieving a goal with all good intentions and climbs strong and skillfully up a tree, but didn't take the time or have the presence of mind to realize he was going up the wrong tree.

## Delight in Truth at all Costs

Everything that is experienced must be accepted. Simply say, yes, this is happening to me. We tend to avoid and repress and choose against less pleasant feelings. What a rip-off! These selfsame unpleasant feelings are important information as to what is going on; they hold the key to why we don't at the moment have pleasant feelings. They are, in fact, the feelings needing the most attention.

Delight in truth at all costs. It is always an opportunity. Validating the truth reveals the way out of the fog and into the light. Stated simply, if you don't know where you are, how can you get to where you'd like to go.

Having said that, it is not always easy to know what the truth is; especially when it has been hidden in denial for a long time. But we mustn't be afraid and must be truth seekers.

One way that the avoidance of truth expresses itself is in the body as pain or discomfort. When a part of your body is complaining or hurting don't just wish it away. And don't blame the messenger. Ask yourself what the message is. Validate what you are feeling and follow the clues.

"Seek and ye shall find." Yeah, right! Well it is right but not always, or even often, easy. But we must stay at it. It is also true that like everything else practice improves our ability. The oftener we seek, the easier and more natural that seeking becomes. Plus as we retrieve more of our truth from the shadows and from denial, the less muck there is to obscure it.

## Don't Get Caught in the Looking for Results Trap

Although it is natural or at least normal for people to rate their existence and their time on earth in terms of results, it can be counterproductive to be looking for results and placing results as the highest priority.

It seems that in the ever accelerating rat race of these modern times that our and many societies have become, action and accomplishment is highlighted. And it seems our fellow rats are moving faster all the time seeking goals that are ever more remote. This cannot be good for the heart and soul, or for our bodies.

From a spiritual viewpoint perhaps having no goals of accomplishments is of more value. Live in and for the moment. Perhaps what's more important is having a good heart and a quiet mind. That, also, should align, strengthen, and heal the body. Seek peace.

I think there is a middle ground. I would agree that there is something to be said for being able to reflect on one's life and feel proud of what you have accomplished. Having goals is not in and of itself destructive; just don't get caught in the looking for results trap. It is all circular. It is ok to value accomplishments but a good heart and a peaceful mind should come first.

I would suggest that having a goal in sight but focusing on the means rather than the end actually makes the accomplishing of goals more likely. Also, part of the trap of looking for results is that if those results are too tightly defined, it may get in the way of having unexpected but equally valuable or more valuable results as the outcome.

## Adopt a Child's View of Life

Watching some children one day something occurred to me; a natural condition of their lives that would naturally give them a life perspective that we as adults have lost. Or maybe I should say, quite literally have grown out of.

Children are quite obviously in a constant state of change. They are growing. Up. On the surface, they take it for granted. Paradoxically, they are very aware of their growth. I'm bigger than I was last year. Next year I'll be as big as older bro or sis is now. Hey, I can reach the lowest branch of that tree and climb it now; I couldn't do that last summer. This offers them the optimism and belief that many things may be achievable in the future that are not now possible. Also skills and talents develop and improve as their bodies' capabilities improve and also as they accumulate experience and exposure to more and more new things.

I think, as adults, we buy into a kind of static situation. We fret that we can't do certain things, thinking, I haven't been able to do that up till now; what reason do I have to believe that will change. We worry about conditions that need not be permanent. Our bodies seem less supple and less responsive to challenges and we accept that. Although there may be certain changes in the exuberance of the bodies we inhabit as adults, I think they are far less restricted than we have come to believe. And, I believe that our attitudes all too often support that belief and probably to a great extent are responsible for the creating of the conditions that make us feel more sluggish in body and spirit. Thus we create self fulfilling prophesies.

Adopt an attitude of openness. Don't buy in to cannot. Even as we may develop conditions that really can't change, as long as there is life there is a place to grow. Seek enthusiasm. Allow what is but assume change. Assume it as a natural quality of life. And give it the benefit of the doubt that the change can be for the better.

## Check it Out: Does This Bring me Pleasure?

What is the meaning of life? What is important? Does this have value? The answer is in another question. Does this bring me pleasure? Does this feel good?

## Reminders

It will be argued that a philosophy of seeking pleasure is a recipe for a hedonistic no good lifestyle. The question is are you up to it? Have you matured yourself enough to recognize real pleasure? Not frivolous behavior that leaves you with a hangover, be it of the body or spirit. That which brings you real pleasure will always be something of value. Cheating and lying may offer you a temporary gain and one might find a corrupted pleasure in that, but the pitfalls and traps are many. That ain't true pleasure.

Things that bring true pleasure have no down sides. Not necessarily no complications or struggles as we unravel ourselves, but you will be enhancing your life and your progress.

How could doing what is right not work? How could doing what really feels good not be good for you. It makes no sense on any level that our hearts and bodies would be so constructed that pleasure would be something to be avoided. Pleasure is simply the smooth functioning of a being.

Try and create a life of things that feel good. Of course in a multifaceted world and society and personal life you can't always do things on your feel good list. Just do the best you can. Say prayers. Be reflective. Don't ever abandon love or loving. Trust in nature.

Become selfless. Give freely. Discover the pleasure of giving.

Become selfish. Hunger for the pleasure of giving.

## Aesthetics and Values Will Carry You When Knowing Can't

Watching college age kids in the park one day I was thinking how you can't expect them or children to really know themselves, to recognize the threads in society and in the world. Most of them simply haven't had enough twists and turns in the road or perhaps the demands of adulthood to have a feeling for how life unfolds. And you can't really expect them to have communication down, to have matured communication in a wide variety of circumstances with others.

Wisdom does come with age. Or actually I should say wisdom can come with age; the passing of years offers more and more opportunity to gain wisdom that can be used for the betterment of all.

But, as I was watching those kids in the park I saw something else. I saw clearly that each one of them has, regardless of age, an innate ability to be aware of aesthetics and values. And it was also clear to me that those really are enough. More than enough, they are necessary. They will carry you when knowing can't. What's more, aesthetics and values will be the vehicle that will transform experience into wisdom.

## Shorty Reminders

✔ Get into it. Get past the cliché. Really get into it. Get inside. Slow time down and get in step with whatever you are doing, seeing, hearing, feeling, smelling, touching, or imagining.

✔ Daydream fantasies. Creative visualization. Trepidation. Fear. Whatever. You are what you think about all day.

✔ Ultimately you can't make someone do something against their will. I'm not sure if I really believe that, but assume that it is true or that you wouldn't want to because it is not right. If you can't make anyone love you, seek out your company, have sex with you, give you money, and so on, what you can do is change your own vibration so it seems desirable for others to find the option of you favorable.

✔ De-crystallize. If you state an opinion, learn something, or make a mistake, there's no reason to feel bad or proud. It's not you. It's just something you did, or said, but you don't own the past and it doesn't own you. It's one of those cool paradoxes though. You can't use that as an excuse to not be responsible. You've just gotta stay free and sensible.

- ✔ Don't be smug because of having things, material or otherwise, in your life. These satisfactions and creature comforts ought to be recognized as the means, not the end.

- ✔ Never believe that what you say is what you communicate. Be aware that what is heard by others when you speak to them isn't necessarily what you said; at least not in meaning or intent. Without being on the same wavelength or in some profound way having worked out a common lexicon based on experience, it's probably an illusion that they have any idea what you truly mean, where you are really coming from in your realm of experience when you put your well chosen favorite words together.

- ✔ Being in a positive space is obviously fertile ground for success. Experience has taught me, however, that there is something more effective. Seek instead to remove the negative, leaving you in a neutral space, where all things naturally take place.

- ✔ Mood and attitude is everything. To try and change the physical first is like the trailer trying to pull the tractor. Or perhaps like the trailer trying to push the tractor.

- ✔ Happiness and loneliness are not necessarily mutually exclusive. It's possible to be happy and still be lonely. A person in a general state of happiness can experience loneliness. Loneliness happens. It's part of the richness of being human.

- ✔ No matter how much you may doubt that you have a worthy talent or skill, it just ain't so. Look high, look low. Don't leave any stone unturned. Don't think anything is insignificant. Get to know your style. Do what you're good at. It looks good on you. It fits you well. It is an opportunity to shine without trying too hard.

- ✔ A place in your heart and soul isn't enough. There must be a place in your life or it isn't happening. Look to your heart and soul for that which you desire, then do what you need to find or make a place in your life for it.

- ✔ Change is inevitable. It is movement and that is the very stuff of life. And since it is inevitable why resist it. That's where the pain starts. If you feel the urge to fight change, take a moment, step back, and see where it is going to the best of your awareness. Realize that change is not only inevitable, but that change itself is good and natural. By first accepting it, this gives you the opportunity to participate in the change and help shape the outcome.

- ✔ Admit the limits of your awareness and senses, ask and pray for magic. Accept it without having to understand it or feel personally responsible for it.

## One Liner Reminders

- ✔ God allows us mistakes to build character. I forget sometimes.

- ✔ When you do it right it's gone, when you do it wrong, it's still there.

- ✔ Happiness is the relation between what one imagines their needs to be and what one imagines to have.

- ✔ Reality is synonymous with power. Relax and expand.

- ✔ If you don't do it, it won't get done.

- ✔ You can't steal 2nd with one foot on 1st.

- ✔ Undirected will becomes frustration.

- ✔ Feel stuck? Feel restless? Go out and make some mistakes today.

- ✔ You can't go swimming by looking at the lake.

- ✔ Want to feel good, instead of wanting something to happen so you will feel good.

- ✔ Fear mustn't be the reason for strength in solitude.

## Reminders

- ✔ All ideas are valid.

- ✔ Life is hard enough without thinking it's hard. Keep moving.

- ✔ Time is yours to live within; on your own terms.

- ✔ Relearn, re-integrate in new applications, under new circumstances.

- ✔ Instead of thinking, "it's like this", think, "that's one element of a bigger picture."

- ✔ Pain is only felt in resistance.

- ✔ Never judge the limits of what you can do, until there's no turning back.

- ✔ Love the process, you can't own anything.

- ✔ How does it feel in your gut?

- ✔ Act with the certainty that you have when the chips are down because hey, the chips are always down.

- ✔ Don't let fear make your decisions for you.

- ✔ Giving is receiving.

- ✔ Appreciate everyone's individual perception.

- ✔ Be true to the best you know, and the next will be given to you.

- ✔ It's ok to make a mistake doing something you feel you need to do.

- ✔ Repeat after me: I am, I can, and I don't have to.

- ✔ Forgive the past, keep clear the present, forgive the past.

- ✔ What you create for yourself, you create for the world. (and visa versa)

- ✔ Be unrealistic. Ask for what you want.

- ✔ Careful, now. Don't get so involved in the physical that you expect it to rescue you.

- ✔ Simplify and be happy. Fewer moving parts; less to go wrong.

- ✔ Be on a mission. Stay in school. Whether your school has walls or not.

- ✔ When a parade blocks your way, the only way to get past is to join in and pretend you're part of it for a while as you work your way to the other side.

- ✔ It's alright to be disappointed in someone. It's not alright to hold them responsible for your disappointment.

- ✔ If you don't know what you know because you know it, you don't really know it.

- ✔ A ship is safe as long as it stays in port, but that's not what ships are built for.

- ✔ Treat your life as an independent force.

- ✔ Not making connections is a sin of the mind.

- ✔ No matter how much pain you may be in, recognize the cosmos and commune.

- ✔ As soon as you are ready to accept something, you don't need to.

- ✔ Unused potential is a morbid thing.

- ✔ He who lives by the sword, dies by the sword. He who lives by the mind, dies by the mind. If you must use your brain, try and wonder about things rather than think about them.

- ✔ If you want to know your future, look at your present and see what survives.

- ✔ The unknown always conditions the known.

- ✔ Believe in yourself.... for Christ's sake.

- ✔ Genius corresponds with enthusiasm; it all opens up.

- ✔ The alignment you have when you express yourself determines the power your expression will have.

- ✔ When you have loosened the winds, you must abide by their blowing.

And finally...

- ✔ Be Excellent To Each Other

# Earth in Peril

## Preface

These writings on our earth in peril consist of ideas, reflections, and feelings on the theme of mistreating our planet. It is about our physical body's home planet, my personal love for it, and a sharing of insights as to why we mistreat it, as well as emotional reactions to what I see happening to the earth.

I was born in Seattle and grew up just north of the city limits which at that time was mostly woods. Growing up playing in the woods, among the evergreens, streams, and swampy meadows, along with the wild huckleberries and the stinging nettles, the appreciation of Nature was a natural thing; something I was a part of - not an intellectualization of ecopolitics. Love of the earth was in my blood as I grew up and lost my innocence and became aware of what was happening to her. As an adult my mind saw it as my body and soul felt it.

Earth in Peril is about ethics and values. But maybe most of all, sensitivity; which is to say awareness of our environment and all that that implies. Our sensitivity to what is going on around us has to do both with how open our physical senses are and with our attitude. At best, neither are biased or numbed by becoming "used to" the way things are; this is hard because we quickly learn to accept and adjust to new conditions; probably an instinctive aid to survival.

When one is sensitive, disharmony is experienced as well as harmony. Sometimes it's difficult, in light of how much disharmony there is now on this planet, to remain sensitive. But I must validate what I observe, what I feel. One reason I choose to stay open is because I have a strong desire to be able to be a little naive and act as if things were in harmony and as if I can take the simple liberty of being free; acting freely. In fact, the words naive and native come from the same Latin root, nativus. Natural.

Although some of the writings do suggest possibilities, this is more from the gut, than it is a preaching of a solution; it is offered to a world in need of taking the time to stop and smell the roses. My hope would be that what I've written will compel the reader to think about how they feel, act on and react to those feelings, ask questions, and speak their truth. Together, as we become more and more fully alive, I believe the Truth will out.

I dedicate Earth in Peril to my parents whose good hearts and integrity gave me the opportunity and freedom to enjoy a childhood free of stress, allowing me to be appreciative of the world and the abundance of Nature around me. And to my brother, who shared it with me.

sun, the earth is turning
it's turning round
and love is the access
but they chop the tree down
- Donovan

## Earth in Peril Contents

Our Relationship With Nature...................................132
Earth Pays The Price For Social Distortion..............139
Behaving Responsibly, Proactively, Communally...146
Dancing (a journal entry)..........................................159
Several Earthy Dreams..............................................164
Lost and Found.........................................................170

# Our Relationship With Nature

When I saw the movie Greystoke it affected me deeply. I lost my (city) self in a green world of primal needs and affections. Of spontaneity and genuineness. Coming out of the theater my car seemed totally alien. I handed over my keys to my friends and left them to drive home without me and took off over land, walking and running home. I ran through a field and stashed my wallet under a log. I couldn't stand feeling it in my pocket. Pulsing with energy and vitality, I felt a million years old. And entirely capable.

Looking at the expanse of the land and the ridge of the Santa Cruz Mountains under the moon's light and then the little boxes people live in, outside seemed so right. So fertile. So Native. Not outside as a place beyond the door, but the earth. Where life really takes place, no matter how much we try and civilize it away.

In nature, emotions seem to have their place in the scheme of things. I have learned that when I'm hurting I can sense how it is part of the process and acknowledge that what I'm feeling is indeed in its right time and right place if I am aware of myself as a part of the planetary community; I mean all life. It helps me honor the reality of those feelings and consequently to come to terms with them.

- - -

Once while traveling in Switzerland I took off above the town I was staying in and climbed; well, hiked and ran actually, up to and all through the woods on the mountain there. Through meadows and woods, as well as trails. I found a place in the sun and warm wind overlooking Lake Zürich.

After California's dryness and brown that I was used to it was divine. It was incredibly peaceful but it also brought into focus how uncontent I really was. Even as I was loving being there I was thinking about going back down, thinking of doing something else.

Another summer, in another place, while visiting friends in Bellingham, Washington, I climbed up Chuckanut Mountain. It was my first day in the area after much driving and I needed some nature. At the very top, a short distance from each other are Pine and Cedar Lakes. They were storybook perfect. Two very small lakes nestled in a dark woods with little underbrush except thick swampy plants and deep green vegetation all around their edges. Devil's club, lily pads, skunk cabbage. Ultra serene. I sat on an old tree that had fallen into the lake and sloped down and into the water. Again, even as I was loving it I was getting antsy. It was almost too much to handle.

Listen to my language. "It was incredibly peaceful but it also brought into focus how uncontent I really am." And "almost too much to handle." How do I just be still?

Is the hurting we do to the planet just a natural by-product of distancing ourselves from it? Has it actual become our enemy? And why, for god's sake? Just because it can't help but try and bring us back home; welcome us back into the fold. It's the only way it knows. It's love. It's harmony. And we can't handle it. There's just too much pain to feel when we're too still for too long.

So we kill the messenger.

- - -

From my window I was watching some kids playing across the street, and I was amazed and appreciative of how they can entertain themselves on a step, in a patch of dirt, almost anywhere. Their physical world is so much smaller. And more immediate. At the same time, their psychic world is so much larger. Adults are just the opposite. Our psychic world is so limited (stunted is probably more accurate) and our physical world, our range, is so much larger.

Could it be we require or think we require so much space and so much in general because we seek that greener grass, searching for the place or thing we will find that will fill the void left by our impaired psychic selves and our slide into density and fear? In our inability to find peace where we are, we seek in one way or another to control. And it is, in the broader sense of the word, always the "environment" we need to control when we feel incapable of dealing with things as they are.

- - -

A favorite piece of jewelry of mine is a necklace with a pentagon shaped jade star on a light chain that I have gotten many compliments for. But once I ran into some guy who laid a trip on me, telling me that it was devil energy because it was pointing down. He intimidated me so much that I didn't wear it for a long time after that. I eventually made peace with it after having given it much consideration and reflection, and had come to the idea that pointing up it was more cosmic and pointing down more earthy. I think he was reflecting the ethics, the beliefs that base and mundane things, that carnal things are evil. It is a cornerstone of so much religion; along with the derision of pagans and heathens. It follows then that association with our baser needs and contact with the primitive and intimate contact with the earth evoke guilt. But since we are of the earth and need that contact we are forced to have a relationship with it, but it is one of disassociation and confusion. Denied the pleasure that is rightfully ours, the earth suffers by misdirected malice as we stoke a false pride in the conquest of our technology over it.

And if I observe myself I can see, thankfully not malice, but that all too often I take much too little time to feel the earth. I'm just barreling along over its surface and through its atmosphere, rarely even aware that I'm breathing.

- - -

There was a stretch of time, a while back, when I was very involved in politics; mostly distributing information about what was really happening. It became very frustrating when I began to realize that people could know of inhumane atrocities and of ecological slaughter and it didn't faze them.

I know that mostly people are good at heart. Why didn't they care?!

One day, while I was riding my bike, I smelled the awful sickening smell of a roof being hot tarred. A block further on, I came across the construction site and I saw something that opened my eyes.

There was a light but steady wind blowing and the thick black smoke from the trailer holding the hot tar was blowing horizontally in one direction away from it. There were two construction workers standing next to the trailer in the path of the smoke, talking. They could have moved several feet in either direction and been virtually free of the smell and effect of the smoke.

My god! It became clear to me that before people react to any "knowing", they must be sensitive enough to feel that it makes any difference. What would be the point in telling these two men that the quality of food they put in their bodies would make any difference?

- - -

I have a tape by a German man named Rene Bardet which is music to the text of Chief Seattle's words in 1855 to the United States president in response to an offer to buy their land. Extremely powerful, it is beautiful, angry, philosophic, and sad. "How can the sky be bought or sold, or the warmth of the earth? This concept is foreign to us. If we don't own the freshness of the air or the glittering of the waters, how can you buy them from us?"

In a book called The Ohlone Way, about the Ohlone Indians who lived in the Santa Cruz area and south San Francisco Bay, it describes the North Central California coastal area and the bays; how it was. Even in summer it was wetter. The water table was higher. There were many deltas and marshes. Birds and wildlife flourished. There were reeds and swamps all along the shores. Reading that one night, it really moved me and hurt me.

I remember seeing in a movie some proud civilized man puffing his chest out and telling about how people like himself, the bold pioneers in America, had come and made this land what it is; part of that being that they had drained the swamps. My god! Even as I write this I shudder. These people went out of their way to drain the swamps! It seems to me these attitudes and acts are more responsible for making this land what it isn't. But what do I know? I suppose a flat earth is much more manageable.

In my head I believe there is a place for "progress" but sometimes in my gut I feel that the only work worth doing is that which undoes civilization and allows the abundance to return. The richness of life.

- - -

A wonderful book I once read was the journals of Lewis and Clark, recounting in much detail their daily adventures; telling of their hunting and foraging and this new (to them) land they were encountering. At one point they wrote of a story told to them of the legend of the origin of the Osage Indians:

> According to universal belief, the founder of the nation was a snail passing a quiet existence along the banks of the Osage, till a high flood swept him down to the Missouri, and left him exposed on the shore. The heat of the sun at length ripened him into a man, but with the change of his nature, he had not forgotten his native seats on the Osage, towards which, he immediately bent his way. He was however soon overtaken by hunger and fatigue, when happily the Great Spirit appeared, and giving him a bow and arrow, showed him how to kill and cook deer, and cover himself with the skin. He then proceeded to his original residence, but as he approached the river, he was met by a beaver, who inquired haughtily who he was, and by what authority he came to disturb his possession. The Osage answered that the river was his own, for he had once lived on its borders. As they stood disputing, the daughter of the beaver came, and

having by her entreaties reconciled her father to this young stranger, it was proposed that the Osage should marry the young beaver, and share with her family the enjoyment of the river. The Osage readily consented, and from this happy union there soon came the village and the nation of the Wabasha, or Osages, who have ever since preserved a pious reverence for their ancestors, abstaining from the chase of the beaver, because in killing that animal, they killed a brother of the Osage. Of late years, however, since the trade with the whites has rendered beaver skins more valuable, the sanctity of these maternal relatives has visibly reduced, and the poor animals have nearly lost all the privileges of kindred.

What a perfect allegory. Human springs forth from nature, forgets its roots, is forced to deal with survival, claims dominance over nature, feminine influence reconciles, human and nature marry and share the earth. Until temptation and greed divorce human and nature and nature is no longer recognized as family.

### Earth in Peril

# Earth Pays The Price For Social Distortion

I saw something while driving one spring that cracked me up. It cracked me up because it was so creepy. Steven King couldn't have done any better. I saw an old woman out on a patch of her lawn by the road, stooped a little, wearing a long overcoat, decapitating dandelions with a long handled scythe type tool. It struck me as such a metaphor for evil. Someone going out of their way to hack off these beautiful yellow flowers in pursuit of some sort of orderliness.

- - -

I used to sometimes tape movies on TV with my VCR and watch them later. One such movie was called I Will Fight No More Forever. A really powerful movie, it is based on the real history of Chief Joseph and the Nez Perce Indians and their reaction and response to white man taking their valley to put it to use; that is, to good white man use. Powerful cinematography. Powerful scenes. Universal soldiers. Conscience of the white man.

Having been taped from a broadcast station there were many commercials. While fast forwarding through them, the images of our Babylon; its perverse sex and obesity and its products evidenced our separation from our source.

I've been using, in my mind, the word Babylon a lot recently in viewing our culture. So much material. Sure it's fine to have comfort, but the rush of gadgetry and, in general, advertising and promotion that attempts to convince and persuade rather than just informing the populace of its availability. And of course this only works because of the buyer's weakness ; it's all taken on so easily. But it just gets harder and harder to get thrills. It takes more and more to get off.

- - -

During the first Gulf War, I heard a sound bite from a politician saying she hoped it would be over soon so we could get on with our normal lives. It really pushed my buttons. For her, normal meant accepting insane greediness and inequity, suppression of truth and ignorance of corporate crime; accepting it into our lives as "the way it is", mimicking and supporting it. I don't mean just paying our taxes and electing corrupt and ingenuous people. I mean supporting the patterns and the values; playing the game, looking out for how it can work for us, without really having to change too much.

We will not stop the destruction by playing their game.

- - -

In a long talk about drugs with some friends in Europe, encountering resistance, I tried to explain that, objectively, we all have choices and make them to satisfy certain things. And certainly more people get fat, sick, and dead from cars than they do from LSD. But the puritanistic emotional factor was too high.

So much fear. We must be open to conceive of all possibilities. I don't in any way, shape or form feel that these people were lacking in their hearts. But, as in similar discussions I have had, I see so much good heartedness and pain together. Denial. So much resistance to sex and drugs and anarchy. And so easily accepted the filth that science whips into our food and our water and our air.

## Earth in Peril

- - -

I once saw an ad on TV promoting: "The healing foods." And saying: "Cures diseases." Probably their heart was in the right place but to say cures or even prevents is bizarre. It's all backwards. All damage control. Without vision. Instead of foods to fight off evil, why not foods to create goodness and harmony in the first place. In the garden of Eden those foods are simply the natural wave that carries you; creating human and natural forces in union, superseding disease.

With stunning clarity and simplicity I see the politics of buying organic food. Every time you buy something inorganic, you are paying someone to poison the earth. Plain and simple. It's just that it's so easy to make destructive choices. It's built into our society and our lifestyle. It's our paradigm. The storefronts look so neat and clean. It's all so spiffy. Hard to believe anything could be amiss in such nice places.

- - -

There is another upside down way we look at food. When you go to a food store, thanks to some government regulations, the ingredients and certain other information about the food is on the label. The information is, to be sure, limited and often misleading, but it is a start.

One of the most important differentiations in food is whether it is "organic" or not. Organic meaning grown free of pesticides and other chemicals. Now, there is some skepticism about whether organic food is really organic and how much different or better for you it is but that's not the point. Let's just assume that organic means it is truly natural.

You plant it and nature with a little assistance from the farmer grows it, it's harvested and shipped to your store.

So what is upside down here? I'll tell you. Much of the reason that organic food is such an elite, in a way, item and that it is considered by so many to be a foolish waste of money, is the lack of knowledge about "normal" food. As it is now you look at produce or packaged products and decide if you want to buy "food" or something labeled as "organic food." In a sane world, in an right side up world, you would go to the store and looking at the labels you would see your choice: "food" or "chemically treated or synthetic food."

I suspect that given that choice, just plain "food", free of tampering would grow in popularity. As it is now, sometimes foods are almost but not all organic and on the ingredients list there will be a asterisk next to each item that is organic. Imagine in a right side up world, no asterisks for organic, but asterisks for chemically treated or synthetic ingredients and an ingredients list being required to list all chemicals used on each product, from the fertilizer, through sprays and the processing.

There is only one problem with this sane idea. There probably isn't enough room on the average label.

- - -

Reflecting on Heaven and a soul's progress after watching TV, I started thinking "man, hell is gonna be packed." The greed and fear manifested in aggression and the consequent destruction is so great now. Perhaps there's always been as much disharmony in the human condition - probably more - but the consequences now are so far reaching. So many facets of our modern life, tucked away unseen, can kill on such a grand scale. Alone the level of

# Earth in Peril

energy that we seem to believe we need could destroy the planet.

There is enough mention of ecology in the press these days that we all know about it but the mainstream message is still just to carry on. Things are fine, really. It's somewhere else those things you hear about are going on.

So what about the huge middle masses who don't intend to hurt, but who are too afraid to risk being an individual or simply not inclined to act out of the ordinary?

I recognize that mostly they are good people. They're not intentionally evil. And yet... so many of their choices are vastly destructive. Something to do with mass agreements and mass denial. Agreement to not challenge each other's comfort zones. And consequently, in the agreement, there is co-ordinated widespread manifestation of that denial. And that resistance to change, when change is absolutely necessary, is deadly.

- - -

Basically banks and insurance companies just exist because people aren't together. And it strikes me that it's just like disease. Disenfranchised cells and body parts make nice homes for cancer, viruses, bacteria. "Hey, here's some material no one is claiming. Let's use it." In society, when people are separate, the lack of cohesive energy flowing between individuals leaves certain areas of life's concerns functioning under par and vulnerable to foreign entities. Parasites thrive. It's only natural; if we don't work together to accomplish that which needs to be done, then some other entity will and probably not in our best interests.

- - -

A friend of mine surprised and discouraged me. He was really getting down on another friend of ours for being 33 and still "bumming" rides. I commented that he was saving the environment and my friend said rides should be paid back with rides. I said there were many ways to be paid for favors, many ways to contribute. He stuck to his rigid idea of sharing.

It disturbed me that people still - what do I mean still?!; it's normal - trash each other because they feel taken advantage of. And in this case the earth pays for the work ethic get-even-ness.

As we tighten our power to create or destroy, thrive or rot, co-ordinated is so powerful. The old patterns of claiming turf against the world are choking us as a community and a species.

- - -

I know that my personal approach is often too bold for some people, but although I stumble and challenge and perhaps intrude, there is goodness. Intrusion is certainly a matter of viewpoint. Status quo and law and normalcy and accepted societal ways is an awesome aggressive intrusion on me, all sensitive people, and the earth.

If the people of the earth were living in harmony with natural law, the "intrusive" (disrupting) environmental protesters and activists would be quietly going about their lives and business, and the people who are now doing business as usual would have to rob land to plunder and would have to take over factories and manufacturing plants, then hold them by force to produce their toxins, split their atoms and build their bombs. In fact, if you really think about it, what they are doing already is robbing land, then trashing that land as they take resources that they have no right to, then using force to suppress any challenge to their "free trade." It's only because society is stupefied into acceding to their business practices that they seem civil and the protesters and activists seem out of line.

I came across this quote in the foreword to a science fiction book. "Anarres, Shevek's homeland, is a bleak moon settled by an anarchic utopian civilization." I found it interesting, that the adjectives "anarchic" and "utopian" were used together. Why not? Most people think of anarchy as being violence and looting and destructive greed driven chaos. I never have thought that lawlessness implies those results. Anarchy is not what you think it is. In fact I maintain that we already have anarchy; of the most insidious kind. Money and politics and police and militaries supported by corrupt laws and legislation do exactly as they please, often with the guise of acting on our behalf, but ultimately using force to protect their destructive rampage.

# Behaving Responsibly, Proactively, Communally

While attending the Sonoma County Supervisor's meetings in Santa Rosa every week as a camera operator, I became increasingly discouraged because they weren't visionary; the way they would address each issue just seemed like damage control. That's all they really sought. For the most part, they'd just do what was necessary to get out of each little bind. Or more accurately, to alleviate the symptoms in each bind.

It struck me that there is a good analogy in sports. I'm always looking for a way to show people that they already know the principle, and if they would just recognize it, then they can apply it.

It's like letting the ball play you; standing flatfooted in the infield and at the last moment having to deal with whatever awkwardness and complications arise. Instead, at the first recognition that a line of human activity exists, one could decide how it would most favorably play out and move to create the proper relationship between the people involved and the activity; play the ball.

I also find that people seem compelled to honor things they create, for better or worse. Maybe it's just hard to admit you made a mistake.

Cars are a great example of both of these phenomena.

There are certainly many ways that what cars do in everyday life, could be done. Mass transit, spatial arrangement of towns more appropriate to carless living, lifestyle adjustments, even altering the pace at which things seem to need to be accomplished. But instead, we let the car play us. It's here, it's an appendage, and it's only when we choke (more accurately, only when our head begins to spin at the last moment before we go under) that we try to do a little something.

So cars have been invented and now it seems that they serve many purposes but who will go back to the roots of those purposes and pretend a car doesn't exist or pretend a car doesn't work (much like someone in their right mind would, who invented something nifty, but had to give it up because they found out it was poisonous) and seek out other inventions or solutions to the problem.

The promise of the automobile seems to lie somewhere right alongside those shorter workweeks and life of ease that technology promised us some decades ago.

Something else. It seems that it's rare that someone takes a quantum leap into a new area of thinking. It's interesting how history works that way. It's another good reason to get out of history and into pure recognition of our nature and our native needs and our most gutsy desires. "What is it?" "What can we do about it?"

It seems to me that there is a kind of natural law that in life you have to face things. If you choose to do so, you can to some extent orchestrate the encounters. If you choose not to face things, they're just going to happen to you anyway, whether or not you're prepared.

- - -

Political action, even when it is little more than damage control, can be a vehicle for consciousness. If you think about recycling and conservation there's no amount that individuals can do which will stop the destruction while it continues to be caused on the scale of that of the government, big business, and industry, if they go on unchecked. But as people perform these humble acts, they grow; consciousness and spirit grow and it will bring the healing.

I wonder if using the word "political" the way I just did might sound a little too heavy and off-putting. I don't think being political, given the entangled mess our country and the world is in right now, is something I can really expect of people. Instead, it occurred to me that it is very reasonable to expect a certain level of "civic responsibility" from people.

- - -

I've been thinking a lot lately of the concept of teamwork as an accessible analogy for people who can't conceive of we are all one. Everything is a part of a system; many smaller systems as parts of one infinite system. The solar system is a system. The earth is a system. Communities are systems. The body is a system.

If you think of the body and its parts functioning together like a football team, there are some interesting analogies. Would any coach put in a player who's just going to sit around. Or how about a player who is renegade and runs the wrong way. We are all coaches of our own bodies and the ground rules are pre-determined by Nature and any tough guy who's ever had anything to do with team sports (even watching) ought to recognize how exactly the same it is.

You can get even more specific. Too much or devalued food can be viewed as a player just sitting around after the ball is hiked. Poisons and various refined foods that strip the body of more than they give it can be viewed as a player taking the ball and running the wrong direction. It's ground that will need to be made up later.

And the same goes for the system of any community. Sometimes it feels good to go, act, do, but if it's in the wrong direction, what's the point. Frivolous consumption or consumption without wisdom is a great example of this. Also destructive work.

- - -

While reading Edgar Cayce on Atlantis and the Atlantean's indulgence in the material I began reflecting on my selfishness and material wealth. Sure I love, but I also want physical things. Possessions. Stereo. Creature comforts. It's a big responsibility to live with technology and to take and have, but live within bounds and keep in touch with divine laws.

Isn't that great. In that sentence "law" becomes a channel, a vehicle, and not a restriction. It's the key to balance, harmony, common sense.

From the United States Declaration of Independence, the declaration that they should be free: "to assume among the powers of the earth, equal Station to which the Laws of Nature and of Nature's God entitle them."

It does not say the Christian God or the Jewish God or the Muslim God. Nor does it say that the equal station that we are due is granted us under the law of any human legislator. It is the Law of Nature and of Nature's God and it seems to me that should these laws be broken, the document isn't worth the hemp it was written on.

A first small olive branch to Nature's God might be to save those gorgeous god given gardens of green giants by allowing humble humans to harvest hemp for peaceful plentiful paper production.

- - -

I have been giving some thought to building a Tesla Coil. It is a principle of Nature that is just overlooked. It's incredible. But I also understand what Tesla did wrong and what he failed to recognize. He learned that a resonant energy could be supplemented to achieve tremendous power at no loss from the source regardless of how much was powered from it.

But he lacked sensitivity to nature's needs. He might have been the guy that blew Atlantis away. On a small scale, his coils could be invaluable, but on a grand scale it's just too disruptive. Somewhere there is a fine line and it takes wisdom to know it. I see it as an interesting blend of male and female principles in physical energy production.

And what exactly is this wisdom? Wisdom would be recognizing that in nature (which is to say always) there are many factors and forces and creatures to be considered, and in all cases we must temper our activities with sensitivity to the scale of our acts.

How much nectar can a bumblebee carry?

- - -

I had a vision once that maybe it is meant to be and actually a good thing that we can't find a free or super cheap non-polluting car fuel. I don't think we posses the wisdom yet to go with it. I think if we had such a fuel it's just too likely that we'd abuse it by increasing our usage of cars. Maybe no air pollution but how many more cars and new roads would we see?! Even tapping natural energy needs to be done with wisdom. For example how many hillsides do we want to see covered with windmills? And we need to realize that even renewable energy usage creates heat as a byproduct. The earth has had a dynamic balance without our advanced technology for so long. How much more heat can the system absorb without being thrown out of balance? Especially at the rate we are forcing change on it. Scale is everything.

- - -

"Growth" is almost universally hailed as being a necessity and the cornerstone of a healthy economy. Not true. Economic growth is at best inevitably doomed and at worst, virtually death energy. The idea that all must grow is an addiction. Borrowing from the future and taking resources as it does is like a heroin addiction. It's something foreign in the system that compels the system to remain in a state that is not natural and does not meet the basic needs of the system. The taking care of physical needs and mutual support facets have been superseded and overridden. "Growth" is a monster that has taken on an energy of its own and become the primary need and hunger.

If you look to Nature as or for an example, what do you see in terms of growth? All animals and plants grow, reach a mature level where they fit their niche in the system, then stop growing. (At least they slow way down. Some trees may thicken and grow some.) From that point on what might be called growth is inner growth. Developing wisdom, efficiency, expertise, and energy towards progeny - a new generation to continue.

Curiously our economy's hunger for continued growth in size neglects all of these. In its being compelled by its primary drive - its addiction - it has no time, awareness, or inclination to grow in wisdom or develop creative ways to take care of needs at a stable physical size. What's more, the level of resource consumption and subsequent dross, and greed, in general, are not taking care of the preparations for the next generation's ability to continue to care for each other.

Similarly, in a personal vein, the paradigm of growth in size has short circuited the individual's personal awareness of the desirability of and sensitivity to the fundamental health of growing in these ways - wisdom, efficiency, expertise - after growing "up." People feel a need for "more." Quantity and mass have replaced quality and flow.

I'm sure one could go on forever with analogies, but really, it's so simple. Nature, being functional, provides an example of healthy growth, its patterns, and scale. And it behooves us to always look to Nature and search our souls (inner quality growth) for solutions that support our health and continuity and happiness. Nature is truly efficient.

- - -

In terms of physical space, it's clear that some creations are dense and demand their own area and volume exclusively. They take up space; something else must yield to them. That is obvious but the concept is also true for that which is less dense.

When I used to live in communal households there was usually a record player in the living room and it was more often than not in use. We were really into music in those days. Usually when an album ended, someone would put on another one. I became aware of the fact that active will always dominate passive. Sometimes I didn't feel like hearing music but I did not have the option of taking the initiative, when a record ended, of putting on silence. To want silence as my choice instead of more music required a conversation and coming to an understanding as a group.

Sometimes when I see destructive technology my gut reaction is that I want it destroyed. Or at least I would like to be able to just wish it away. What about being passive? Maybe it is our role as evolved psychic beings to not be totally passive. But of course, the whole point of those in fear is to claim space and not share it, to claim turf, and for us to destroy with physical means would leave their power to do it again intact. It seems our work would have to be a creation of undoing; to psychically recreate the space so it can't be occupied by dense unyielding matter.

It is time to join our powers and to come to that understanding as a group, to create and evolve psychic technology that allows room for humbler creations. I believe it is possible to have flexible creations that are more ethereal and participate with and among others without crowding out and consequently dominating.

- - -

At the post office, while hanging out in line, being appropriately uncomfortable and separate from all the others, none of who were communicating with each other, I imagined saying something in German, then fantasized that a woman ahead of me in line would understand. Suddenly I had this image of each of the heads of all the individuals around me being storehouses of hidden talents, information, knowledge! And just to see them you don't know. To them it could be no big deal. Like, "sure, I speak fluent Swahili." Or, "sure, I spent six months in Nepal. Big deal." But to others it might be a big deal! Think of the information that could be shared. And of the interests that could be shared. And maybe more importantly, think of the inspiration that might come. Someone might have just the puzzle piece someone else has been looking for - if they only knew.

In a similar vein I have this idea of a library of ideas for the new age. A place to be accessed by creative people after the collapse. And a place for people in particular who want to participate in and help create a paradise on this planet but who aren't heard and don't get validation and feel helpless to make any difference. So many ideas. There's probably somebody somewhere with the solution for every problem, if we only knew. It would be a place to register ideas as well as access them when the time has come that the old ways are commonly acknowledged as destructive and the world finally must look ahead; way ahead; ahead to ideas that are out of time and out of style and in harmony and in love.

I am inspired to establish a free idea and invention bank. The tricky part is that it probably will be taken advantage of. It would seem maybe ok with me if somebody takes an idea and makes money off of it, as long as they don't and can't, in the process, claim it and prevent the community from also using it and going further with it. Maybe citizen Hugh Mankind can copyright or patent all the ideas.

- - -

A European friend of mine commented on something I once wrote: If you don't commit, you're just taking up space. She said that she felt it could induce a feeling of guilt if you're not being active in the environmental movement.

Which could then lead to a sense of failure and basically giving up altogether, or feeling despondent. Like there is nothing you can do that is going to matter against the great hypnosis of blind consumption and waste and its consequent dross, so why bother.

I think it's important to say here that commitment can mean many things. We, in simply being alive, are having some sort of impact. And I do believe that being aware of the consequences of our impact is important. But commitment doesn't have to mean action like spiking trees, or lying down in front of a bulldozer, or even writing representatives or voting. Commitment can be sharing our feelings with friends and people we meet about how things are. Or it can be meditating. Or exuding love energy and appreciation while walking in Nature or taking a deep breath of fresh air. There is energy in our attitudes and orientation. Just being focused on what we believe has the power to effect change.

So, being committed means just being awake and aware and allowing your mind and heart to be voices and forces in how you live. As far as just taking up space, yeah, I think if you are content being hypnotized and making choices to avoid the complexity of life, you are just taking up space.

And, if you have guilt around that statement, well, maybe that's what guilt is for. To eat away at us a little and tell us that some part of ourselves is not satisfied with where we're at.

- - -

Thinking about the race to attain health and happiness on earth against the polluting forces, I have felt sadness that some pollutants, especially nuclear, will be around for so long. Then it came to me clearly that with enough beings knowing psychic ecology, the creative energy would be available for a mass purification. In fact, the volatility of nuclear products make them easier to dissipate. Together and living consecrated lives we can recreate a beautiful earth for remaining sojourns of distillation of being.

Yes, the 21st century will be host to the clean-up generations on earth. It won't be just a period of time for many beings to physically clean up the wasted earth. It will also be a time to manifest creativity. Both physically and psychically. A chance to create and a chance to use focused intent and group power to bring about change for the better in exciting new ways.

- - -

I was looking at an article about the growing number of people out of work having the blues for Christmas. I got to thinking about my community share idea; how neighborhoods could share many infrequently used non-personal things. And how by being less consumptive more businesses would thin out. It's just so simple.

Right now everyone thinks they need full time work to get by. If many things were shared, part time work would suffice and instead of laying off 10, 20, 30% of a work force, a company could cut everyone's hours back 10, 20, 30%. In fact, as I think about it, it strikes me how crude it is that companies don't always do that. Certainly there might be some key positions that might need to remain intact, but mostly it's a doable win win and it's how we naturally find the right scale of our activities and our demands on natural resources.

And again, the feeling of a team. If all of a factory's workers were cut back 25%, as members of the same community (meaning all in the same boat) they could work out help for each other.

- - -

The bad economic news can be scary but every time I hear or read these things it just seems like the solution is so simple. Community. Sharing, trading. Less things, more helping. Barn raisings instead of bank loans. Occupations that have meaning. Working for life; not for death. Effort for freedom and personal power; not effort to support each other's addictions.

The word "economy" carries such a stigma but really it's just "how we arrange our mutual support systems." I think that is a pretty good definition and recognizes its potential to be raised.

There are so many people who want peace, who ache for just living and loving their families and friends; if only they weren't afraid. Afraid someone would take advantage of them, afraid they simply won't survive; food and shelter. Afraid they'll be left (alone).

Yes I thrill at the collapse of the current economic style. The transition will be tough, but god it will be validating and heartwarming to be doing business on a smaller scale, exchanging with people, helping each other, thanking each other, and giving up a little to help each other when necessary.

Yeah, big big stuff is coming.

Big big stuff.

Like nothing you've ever seen.

People will have to begin to trade with each other.

Simplicity's virtues will shine.

Local commerce will thrive.
Appropriate technology won't be buried or bought out.
Individuals will heed their creativity.

I'm excited. The master's head's blown off. A fresh wind blows against the empire.

- - -

I ran into a friend the other day and we started talking about where we were going and he started talking about taking the high road. And about people doing what feels good. It struck me that that is so primitive but so true. You can talk about going to Heaven forever but unless you can show people how good it feels on the road to Heaven, they'll get off on cheap highs.

- - -

The time has come to face the music. We gotta start running so much love. The earth must soon be sanctified, 'cause if we just play the matter game; well... take a look around.

Earth in Peril

# Dancing (a journal entry)

I'm back home, after having just seen the movie Dances With Wolves. I'm beginning to understand my predicament. Unfortunately, not the solution. I feel like I could be nearing the end of Roger Brown, Golden or otherwise.

I realized on the walkrun home why I'm not connecting with and reaching people. I have failed to properly impress people with how deeply I am not of this culture.

Coming home I ran from one dark area to the next dark area, the street lights seeming so harsh.

Before the movie, after realizing that Russ and Kim's land, where I am welcome and have considered living, is still way too close to "White man" for me, I felt like putting out a call for a woman who wants to accompany me to live as Indians, deeply natural, far from this madness.

On the walk home I struggled with the style I could make peace with. My work - computer and filing cabinet? Rock & roll and electricity? Perhaps time deeply natural and other time in society. Maybe living in some other culture could be a major part of my life.

The movie also reminded me of my deep sensitivity and how I feel that I am very rarely understood because there are, I believe, so few who are not tourists in nature and tourists in fiction and tourists in art.

When I go to Austria I'm all there.

When I go to nature I'm all there.

When I was with Janne, feeling such deep love and affection, without it having to imply ongoing commitment, I was all there. She was so overwhelmed, I think, because she couldn't imagine something between forever love and tourist loving.

I cried many times in the movie. I cried deeply coming home because the savage wound that the city is, is still open and the indoctrinated children are still left unattended running carelessly amok with the weapon.

I came up with the concept today of "indoctrinated children." When I look down on humans; unaware, smug, hurting themselves and each other, blundering, I see them as and think of them as children. But that is confused with the beauty of children. Indoctrinated children fight over consumer products.

Heavy scene when Smiles a Lot killed and grew up - sort of.

It hurt me to think of their shortsightedness. On the verge of being totally eradicated by white man, the Indians fought each other.

It made me think of the L.A. Rodney King riots this week. Sure everyone else is to blame, but also the inner city blacks themselves. Nearly 30 years after Selma, Alabama, they are still their own enemy. Sure it's hard, but still. It's kind of like the feminists looking for a male solution. The blacks are looking for a white solution. Why should they see any more clearly than the masses drugged on matter, that even if they gain equal privilege in a consumer society, what then?

And also, don't they understand that they are the slaves that made our affluence possible and if they want a piece of this pie we're gonna have to bake more at the expense of some other slaves.

Once again a film has magically come into my life with perfect timing. I was feeling so Indian today.

But I just don't know if I can make the leap alone. Is there some woman out there at the end of her city rope who I could leap with.

Lieutenant Dunbar had a community to take him in when he became Dances With Wolves. I have none. At least none that I know of. And it's more complicated now. Not just because of technology and TV and garden vegetables.

It's more complicated now because it's clear that fighting is wrong and the male-female roles were wrong and societal indoctrination is wrong. There are a myriad souls slowly but slowly dropping out (turning on, tuning in, and dropping out), all with pieces of the truth. And new societies will be so rough for some time to come. Or, well, maybe rough or small. The Higher, The Fewer.

I wonder what it is like for the Indians who acted in the movie to see Hollywood bring alive images of them roaming open unfenced plains and living naturally in their community, playing games, teasing, wearing leather clothes and living without cars or electricity when in reality they're probably lucky to have allotted to them fresh water. And certainly the joy and intimacy of the community is gone. At least I would think so.

I wonder if it is somehow an ironic inspiration and reminder. Like telling a friend about yourself so they can give you feedback and help you see yourself more clearly.

I wonder if there will be a re-communing of natural living Indians in the Americas and if so what form their society will take. Alas, I'm afraid it will be some time before natural communities can really thrive again in the Americas.

It is kind of strange how the development on an individual level seems so even across the land. I doubt there is yet any community in the US where a contiguous group of neighbors are ready to say: My fences are coming down. I cede my land to the greater good. I don't fear I will come out on the short end of the stick.

No wonder. How often when people buy land do they buy because they like or feel good about the neighbors? It's mostly a kind of 1st chakra family survival thing; claiming turf and taking a stand.

What would my name be if I were named for what I am or how I appear? What would a community of people who knew and understood me call me?

Tonight I was seeing how time with Edi and the pace I lived last summer in the Alps has really created a hard act to follow.

I think I am maybe experiencing a culture shock that won't go away.

Now I'm struggling to tidy up my affairs to move on.

Maybe my death fears before going to Europe last year were a recognition that I was about to die as an American consumer. About to die as a daily car driver. About to die as a predominantly money for survival oriented person.

It's kind of like the last time I read Starseed Transmissions, I felt I was at the end of my history in spirit, and I flew until I crashed on concepts of being out of history and free. Crashed because I was still dependent on the mainstream cultures. Now to complete it; or at least move towards that completion, I must shed the trappings of that history.

What have they done to the earth?
When the music's over
Turn out the lights.
It's all music.
Everything is broken up and dances.
All the magic of life, all the diversity weaving, it's all the music of creation.
And they chop the tree down.
When they've killed it all, when all the magic has been replaced by more efficient tools, turn out the lights.

## Several Earthy Dreams

One morning I woke up to the loud noises of logging. I had dreamt that the volume of the noise broke all the windows in the greenhouse.

- - -

I was in a house - one level above the Lake Forest Park house (the house I grew up in) - but it was like on a ridge in Seattle where Alex and Eric live, viewing the Cascades. I got up early and there was an incredible dawn. Pastels hanging around. The mountains were the clearest, most present, and seemed closer than ever before. I wanted to wake everyone and let them see it but I didn't. They were up shortly but when we looked - big disappointment. There was lots of haze and kind of a dark haze coming up out of the valleys. Somebody said it was pollution from the city settled in the valleys and rising. I also checked out the Mount Rainier view. I could just barely see it over the fountain at the University of Washington. I tried a different view and there were billboards in the way. I moved over some, then more, and it was frustrating because billboards kept being in the way.

- - -

I and several friends were on a hilly sloping area. Grassy mostly, with woods nearby, all around, in the lower moister areas. We were atop several large redwood stumps. There were small holes at their cores and I dropped something down one. A long wait, then I could hear a splash. A couple of others tried it on different stumps. Then we were looking around and saw a grove of humongous redwood stumps which were like 20-25 feet in diameter.

We all went over to the biggest and it had openings in it with water, which were several feet across. We sat around and had bunches of toys. Plastic and stuffed Disney characters. I discovered if I threw one in really hard it would bob back up with enough force to pop out of the water a couple feet and I could catch it. I did it a few times and everyone enjoyed watching.

Then we were told not to play there. And I was 20 feet away and someone commented; saying something like how they wouldn't just let kids play there but if they'd gone at tour time or bought tickets or something official they could. This person also noticed the lower halves of my pants legs were soaked in blue ink. So I decided to wash my hands first (which also had ink on them), then go home and change my pants.

I walked into a food co-op; a small juice bar type place. The man in there recognized me and was casual as I walked in and washed my hands. A scene of a man (my age) coming down some side road to the co-op while I was there. He was very alone. Then I was out on the street heading home. On a country road. I was walking along (maybe running) when I became aware of movement in the sky. I felt an incredible sense of foreboding. The feeling you get when it gets suddenly dark and heavy as a storm rushes in. Looking up and simultaneously running into the brush off to the side of the road, I saw a plane flying over, going back the way I'd come. It was a small private type plane. Very wispy and light. Simultaneously on each side of it there were currents and swirls of air, and clouds moved symmetrically on each side and then a sudden crescendo of angels' voices (a whole chorus) like a Christmas chorale. I've hardly ever felt anything - dream or otherwise - as powerful as those angel voices in that sudden crescendo.

The plane spun in the air, some distance away, and apparently crashed. I waited for sound to verify it but didn't hear anything. Then I saw light and heat rising in a shaft, then mushrooming. It scared the shit out of me. I started running towards town, away from it, still looking back and seeing it though. I checked the wind and it was blowing towards the crash so I had a slight advantage.

I felt so incredibly alone; wanting to be with friends.

I encountered Maria and Ed and their kids (real people who live across the street from where I live) and showed them. They looked out the window and saw it. We turned on the radio and it was music, not alert broadcasting, but we weren't convinced. You could still see a shaft of alternating tubes of light rising and mushrooming out.

I ran on to find dearer friends. I came to the front end of a dome car and realized I was on a train. I was a little sorry but we were rushing forward. I was feeling a little of the warm feeling I used to have riding trains as a teenager, rolling through back streets of towns in the East. Kind of secure and separate, able to just observe a hint of other people's reality.

So I went back to Maria and Ed and the kids at the back of the car.

I awoke with a cold streak in my heart. Wondering if it was a premonition, or if it had happened somewhere and in a half wake state asking, begging humanity to be aware of what could happen, and rid ourselves of all nuclear weapons. I thought of The House at Pooneil Corners.

Terrifying. Absolutely terrifying. It's getting light out now, so I think I'll just get up soon. The sound of the angels was so powerful.

Wow - I can only hope it was just my dream.

From here to Heaven is a scar

Dead Center

Deep as Death

All the Idiots have left

God, how can we expect to take care of ourselves in eternity if we can't even take care of the earth and each other here.

It seems like the plastic toys and Disney characters part symbolizes the way, in these times, that entertainment and diversions keep us from what's really happening. In a grove of redwood stumps, we're playing with toys. In denial of the reality of the wasteland.

And the part about the tour tickets is really intense. The kids are not allowed to just play. Their native needs to be spontaneously alive in nature are not allowed. Their only access to it is after somebody has co-opted it, packaged it, and then sells it back to them in a most distorted form.

- - -

The first night after I began compiling Earth in Peril, I had this dream:

Earth is doomed to destruction. Scientists underground are working on it. In many places. Somewhere, by himself, I observe an old amiable Chinese man with eccentric theories and approach, working on it alone. The other scientists tell me to get out of the way. I see how there are ways. The scientists are stuck at manipulating causal links they're familiar with. Working hard but not much vision or sensitivity.

I see how some electrostatic change in the area surrounding the entire planet or some such radical thing can do it.

The dooming thing seems to be an atomic threat but I'm not sure.

I had been in many different places underground tinkering with possible solutions and observing. There was also some sense of panic; it's getting critical.

Then it seems I'm floating in blackness and I hear this faint, yet clear distant voice call to me and say, "I'm from the future." I get a rush; a flush and am ecstatically excited but still in a kind of serene stasis; field. Still in blackness. I'm a little uncertain, but think, yes, I'm being given an answer from a knowing spirit. I say "yes." The voice comes closer and I sense the being coming closer. I realize it's my friend Dan. And probably not from the future. I'm not disappointed. I feel warmth, love, affection, and wisdom.

Still floating, we are part of a chain of people of all races and countries and tribes, holding hands, unified to heal the planet. It's beyond beautiful. It's incredibly right. And it is the answer.

One of the two people I'm holding hands with is Rusty. I'm not sure about the other. It seems it was a woman at one point, maybe, not sure, dark skinned.

I think at one point that it is so petty for me to worry in my life about my desire for a woman. This is so much more important and so right.

A tone becomes audible that I, it seems, had unwittingly started. It seems it was more from my chest and not my vocal chords. A pure clear tone. It grows in volume. Others join.

It seems many use their voices for the tone, which is less powerful. Good intentions but a lower vibe. Still, it's deep and powerful.

It's so far reaching and all encompassing. I'm not sure but I think I started it and am at the center of it.

Then the circle breaks up. Only because we're human. We'll get together and do it again soon. But I'm disappointed. I was prepared to and had thought this would go on until the work was done and the earth saved. My human needs seemed suspended and I could have gone on like that forever.

Still, it's a beautiful scene. It's like a huge area full of people milling about greeting each other and hugging. Really hugging. Long holding each other hugs.

## Lost and Found

In the forest lurk the elves.
Keep an eye out.
In the forest, it's dark and damp.
And kinda creepy.
      But don't worry.
In the forest, reigns perfect chance.
You might find some roots.
In the forest, there's springs and falls.
It's really dangerous.
      But don't worry.

(Because death in the forest is better
      than life on the streets)

Deep in the forest, time flows still.
You can feel that.
Deep in the forest, it's hot and cool.
Quiet sounds loud.
      But don't worry.
On the mountainsides, or in the vales...
My God, there's a snake!
In the trees, or floating in the air...
What was that?!
      Just don't worry.

(Because there's no way out... you're surrounded)

## Earth in Peril

Everywhere in the forest, there's decay.
Look close, it's alive!
Everywhere in the forest looks new.
It's old as the hills.
    So don't hurry.
All over in the forest, life is tangled.
Listen to its order.
All over in the forest, it's sweet and flower.
You can smell your past.
    So don't worry.

(Because now you're really lost... you're almost home)

# True Stories

## True stories from the pen and life of Roger Brown

I would like to extend thanks to all my friends and lovers who supported me and who were there to listen to me retell my adventures and comfort me afterwards.

These stories are just a few of the many I could tell. All of these stories are ones that are recorded in my journals. I have added some details from memory that I didn't write into my journals at the time they happened, but they are, in essence, all true. I don't suspect these are that special or unique, but I thought I ought to compile a few of them because there is in all of them food for the truth seeker; adventure and fellow travelers.

The quest for truth must include social experience, whether it is learning directly from others or learning from the mirror others offer. Or simply observing what different realities there are out there which offer food for thought. Serendipity has always fascinated me. I don't like to take things for granted.

## True Stories Contents

Accidents..................................................................173
Outsiders..................................................................184
Memorable People......................................................194
Events And Adventures...............................................202
Messages From The Universe.....................................220

# Accidents

Over a period of several years, I was present at the scene of a variety of vehicular accidents. Often I was the first, one of the first, or the only person to arrive. It seemed each time that I responded naturally, being fully alive, and acting without the reservation and doubt that seems to typify most of my life. It's like when the chips are down, I'm there.

## Rodriguez I

It was June of 1983. Santa Cruz, California. A Saturday night. It had been a day of feeling so together, yet feeling a little frustrated and restless for all of us. What's holding us back from really living rhythm; from being united and together?

People are so good.

And yet... so naive. - so naive.

It was late - midnightish. I was home, alone in my room. The stillness was broken by squealing tires and a thunk. I ran up the stairs that lead out of my room, out of the house, past the corner house on our cul-de-sac street, and down Rodriguez Street in the direction of the sound. I arrived and found a young woman who was not hurt badly but freaked out. She was high on alcohol. She had gone off the road and hit a large rock, probably at a low speed. I comforted and consoled her. Others who arrived on the scene were weird, I thought; asking her lots of questions when she just wanted to collect herself. Apparently someone called for help because some medics came. They were efficient but so hard.

The other people there just seemed out of their element and the medics were doing what they were trained to do, but none of them seemed to be able to simply grok what it was that was happening and needed. Something a little more personal.

## Rodriguez II

It was June of 1983. Santa Cruz, California. A Friday night. Stranger than fiction. Lying in bed, close to sleep, at 1:30 a.m., I heard skidding tires and a large thud. It was so close to exactly the same sound as I had heard the previous Saturday night, 6 days before. Amazing. I pulled on my pants and shirt and ran down the street. Again. As I rounded the corner onto Rodriguez I could see that no one else was at the scene. I didn't know what I'd find. It occurred to me that I hadn't called 911.

I got there and saw that a car had come down Paul Minnie Street, which T's into Rodriguez, and gone straight through the intersection and into one of several large rocks which some homeowners with foresight had placed between the street and their yard. The woman inside was unhurt, not in shock, except matter-of-factly bummed out about it all.

A police car just happened to be coming down the road as I approached. They called a tow truck. The woman, Juanita, had no money so I lent her $35 so her car could be towed to our house. After seeing that everything was ok, the police left. While waiting for the tow truck to come, I went back home and woke up my roommate, Pam, to come back with me to help make Juanita feel comfortable accepting our house to stay at, since she was from Watsonville, 15 miles away.

Juanita came back to our house. Pam and I and Juanita were all tired but in good spirits. She called a friend to come and get her, though it seemed uncertain how soon he would be able to get there.

After waiting for a while, hanging out in the living room, it was beginning to look like her friend wasn't coming till the next morning. I offered her my sleeping bag and she accepted and laid down. I held out a hand to say goodnight and she took it and held it tightly. We talked a couple minutes then she put her face to my arm and drifted off. It felt nice to help.

## Wendy

November 2, 1983
I had been out riding my bike around Santa Cruz.
Feeling low.
Unhappy with the world; humanity on the run.
Feeling so sensitive - so much madness.

Never in my 3 years in Santa Cruz had I seen or heard so much automobile expression of pain and repression, as during the previous several days. Over and over, many times a day, squealing tires. I saw a car blast up to 50 or 60 down a narrow, one block long, potholed neighborhood street. Insane.

At the corner of Paul Minnie and Frontage Road I came upon a woman on the street. She had been hit on her bike by a truck. Emergency people were there. They and the police were, this time, friendly. I knelt by her and touched her heart a short time. She was in much pain and really scared. Both of her legs were injured.

Oh God.

After they took her away I rode up to the hospital. She was about to go into surgery.

I decided to try and see her again later. She seemed like a healthy beautiful person. Like why? What warning had she missed? And the person who hit her seemed good. Why?

The accident added to my already moody, deeply sensitive day; wondering what my role in this great play might be. Maybe instead of visions of grandeur about changing the world with something grand new, I felt I needed to or should just do something directed, clear, clean, well and help calm.

Christ.

The next day I visited Wendy in the hospital. It's amazing how people adjust. She had had both legs operated on and had pins put in one ankle. And she was doing ok.

I felt so helpless.

Christ, can't I direct my potential somehow?

Later, lying in bed, thinking of Wendy, I realized how true it is that feeling helpless is little good. Praying for her and feeling helpless is so weak. Got to believe, have faith, and send it out there. Maybe in such a sensitive, feeling phase, I was feeling it all. And the helplessness is no doubt such a big part of low faith, being on the run and hunt.

## Old San Jose Road - Head On

March 27, 1986

I lived for a while in a house in the country off of Old San Jose Road, outside of Santa Cruz. I had a shop space in an open shed outside, near the house. While working in the shop I heard a tremendous screech, then a crunch; that crunch sound that is the unique awful sound of car metal being crumpled. It sounded pretty bad. I ran down my driveway and up onto the road really fast. Head on collision. 3 of the 4 people in the 2 cars were hurt. An intense scene. I spent 20 minutes or more just being with one woman, who was the passenger in what I perceived to be the car that was not responsible for the accident. It looked as though they were coming around the outside of the blind curve there and I'm sure had had virtually no time to see the other car. She had a broken arm, face cuts, and lots of pain, but mostly she was very scared, and never knew what hit her. She couldn't figure out why she was there.

I was there for her and it was intense. I didn't feel I had much to give or could be much of a channel. I was just doing it. It was intense for me to think how one moment could change a life. Like her face cuts might have left her scarred and changed her psychology radically for the rest of her life.

The driver of the car she was in had a hurt leg but got out and walked around. I think he was physically fine but he was probably in shock. He had no idea what was going on. I never did find out what happened to the people in the other car. One of them was out walking around, wailing for a minute or two until somebody got him to lie down. Somebody said he had a really bad cut or hole in his head.

A day or two later, I heard from someone, 2nd or 3rd hand that somebody in that accident had died. I wondered if it was that man. I never did follow up and find out for sure.

## Woman and Daughter

April 28, 1988

In Santa Cruz I was driving on Ocean Street and while stopped at a light at Water Street I saw an accident up ahead. Driving on, I saw people running in the County Building parking lot. It turns out that the people in one of the 2 cars had just split.

I passed the cars and it was pretty bad. A woman was on the street shaking. I stopped. Though there were many people around already, I was compelled to go to her and help. Someone had placed a blanket over her. But no one was touching her. Bizarre. Here was a person deep in a radically needy space and no one understands the comfort of touch.

I held her head and talked to her.

She wasn't in too bad of shape. There was a young (maybe 4 or 5 years old) girl standing a few feet away, crying. I asked her if that was her mommy. She said yes. I had her come over and hold her mommy's hand. It seemed like such a simple obvious thing to bring them together for each other. I was amazed no one else had done that.

It felt like they both really calmed in the 5 minutes I was there.

As has always been the case at the accident sites, I have been able to be present for the injured people without being in the way of the emergency people and they have allowed me to remain.

## Two Motorcycles

May 13, 1990

I was on my way to go to a softball game one Sunday in May in Santa Rosa when I saw that a person was down on the road, his motorcycle nearby. There were a couple of other people there but I was one of the first on the scene. It took me a second to comprehend that there was another injured person across the road who had also been involved in the accident; also on a motorcycle. That seemed like it must be a very rare occurrence. A double motorcycle accident. One of them was a teenage boy in lots of pain and fear. He said both his knees hurt and the back of his head.

There was a young woman at the scene who was with a boyfriend. As soon as the emergency people got there he wanted to leave and she really wanted to stay. He seemed uncomfortable. I sensed she was giving a lot of feminine support healing energy, even a short distance away from the injured people. She kept saying she wanted to stay, continuing to look towards the accident scene and attempting to shrug him off. He kept bugging her and finally practically dragged her away. What an insensitive controlling dolt.

The other rider was also in bad but not critical shape.

It really put me through some changes.

I had just come from visiting a friend, Nez, who has a type of cancer. He had gotten into lots of talking and had told me all about the macrobiotic thing he had begun and his cancer theories and his compulsive behaviors and attitudes. Like he really needed to say it and share it.

Yet earlier in the day I had found out from a friend that Arthur, a man I knew from occasional gatherings, who was deformed, was not congenitally deformed, as I had guessed, but that it came from a car accident and I felt deeply how hard it must be to adjust; wanting friends, love, women and not being able to participate like he had been able to or offer what he may have previously.

## Rt. 116

August 28, 1990

I had just spent 2 weeks visiting my mother in southern California, during which time I had read Starseed Transmissions, which had had a profound effect on me; energizing me to be alive. On the way back up north, I stopped in Santa Cruz, visiting my two friends, Karin and Barry, and now they were with me, driving up to my house in Sebastopol. Our first destination, before my house, was to visit my friend Keith, just off of Rt. 116. We were almost to Keith's, almost home, when we came across an accident where the passing lanes are on 116. I stopped and went out to help. Motorcycle accident. There was a man with a head wound who already had 2 people with him and a woman with 2 broken arms and a broken leg. I went to her. She was really scared and mostly in a lot of pain. It was an intense scene. A helicopter was there, landed in a field by the road. Several emergency crews were on the scene. Their work was slow and complicated. The woman I was with knew who she was but not where she was. I talked to her a lot and held her head and hand. I engaged her eyes and kept her company that way; really trying to keep her calm and strong and just passing time till they could medicate her for the pain, which they couldn't do for a long time until they were certain about the injuries.

I really felt like I was doing what I'm here for.

I was really stunned afterwards and Bob (Keith's roommate) was very nurturing at his and Keith's house. I took a shower and felt a little fresher.

Before falling asleep that night, I slipped into concern and hurt for her and had to pull up and out of it to be fresh enough to get some vital quality sleep.

I visited her the next day. She was out of it - drugged - but grateful to be alive and grateful to me. She said "you've got some kind of caring eyes." And told me they think her leg will heal fine, although they still needed to operate the next day and put a pin in so it would hold.

Her parents were there. They had flown out right away from somewhere back east, Michigan, I think. Apparently she had told them about me. They thanked me for doing what I did.

So.... that was my welcome back.

I prayed for Laura Hurwitz.

I feel that the accident was a real healing and blessing for me. It peaked my sincerity and loving as I came home charged into the company of peers after a kind of inward time while visiting down south.

## Rt. 116 - Passing By

February 4, 1991

It was February, at almost the same place on Rt. 116 as the other accident I had stopped at, 5 months earlier. This accident I didn't stop at. I had written in my journal that day, "I seem to be in curious place of solidness of self and sensitivity to others, in a way." I drove slowly by. It was a pretty bad wreck. A rescue guy was in the drivers seat working on someone - perhaps too hurt to move or trapped, the car was so crumpled. A steady rain was falling. I was moved and thought how this was such a major life event and so painful and scary for someone or someones. Then it just came up, like a couple of weeks earlier, when I had heard that the Gulf War had broken out, I started sobbing, crying intensely for a couple of moments. I felt so connected. Not really to that person but really like hurt for painful human drama, like we really are all one and a part of us is suffering. I want us to be healthy.

## Accident Drama

August 20, 1992

Summer. I was living in Bellingham, Washington. Walking, I came upon an odd scene on Railroad Street. It is a street that is one way each side of some old railroad tracks. In that particular block there are a number of taverns. I usually avoided walking that street because the energy is so alcoholic and uncomfortable to me. There were lots of people who appeared to be tavern goers hanging around on the sidewalk and in the street. As I got closer I saw that some sort of accident had occurred. Someone was down on the street. My heart really opened and I wanted to do a big healing circle, but I was surrounded by alcoholics. What a bizarre scene. I felt so sad that the 30-40 people there, looking on, couldn't come together and heal. I tried to do some alone. All around me, weird flat energy, dumbly observing an "accident," a painful drama, and staying shut down. What an odd experience.

It affected me subtly, but profoundly.

- - -

Yes, it's like when the chips are down, I'm there. I have recognized that and wondered why I can't live my life like the chips are always down.

# Outsiders

### No Money, No Shoes

December 17, 1981

Santa Cruz, California

It was sometime in the evening, after dark, and I was driving near the cliffs in town when I spotted a hitch-hiker and figured I might as well give him a ride. I was just driving across town but he appealed to me to take him home, over the mountain to Los Gatos. I couldn't just drop him off and leave him to the night, given the condition he was in, so I took him home. He was limping a little and didn't look very good. He was also barefoot. He told me that he had just come up from the beach where he had had a rendezvous with his ex. They had argued, so his story went, and she had taken his wallet. He had no money and somehow he had also lost his shoes. He was really down. He had recently gotten out of the hospital, after having been there for over a year. He had been hit on a motorcycle by a drunk. He said he was dead for 22 minutes. I felt pretty even and easy to be a piece of good luck in his life. I tried to send him some reassuring energy before I left him.

### Woman Hitch-hiker

December 12, 1985

Santa Cruz, California

It had been kind of strange weird day that seemed to just pass me by. My head felt like it was on crooked and there was pressure. I had that kind of a subtle winter separateness psychotic feeling.

I was driving in town and I phantasized a woman hitch-hiker and becoming friendly.

Well, the first part came true. I did pick up a woman hitch-hiking. She was not very stable mentally. I felt sad and sorry. She was in touch with the practical things; at least she knew her way around and what was going on but her mind was lost in a whirl of human drama. Her voice wasn't clear so I didn't understand all of it but bits and pieces of her childhood, sister, mom, hospitals, institutions, friends, and death. Once she told me a story and laughed that someone went and got a welfare check and came home and his wife had been killed on a moped. She laughed seemingly at the irony of scoring this nice thing just to face its meaninglessness.

## Indian Frankenstein

March 31, 1988

It was a nice spring day and I was really enjoying a slow cruise through the Santa Cruz mountains on the back roads listening to a tape. I felt really peaceful and was really appreciating the beauty.

At the top of Old San Jose Road I came upon a hitch-hiker. I wondered about stopping. I was feeling so mellow and he didn't look very attractive to me. But I thought to myself, "I can't think of any reason not to give him a ride." So I pulled over and did give him a ride and immediately found a reason. He smelled really bad. And seemed pretty lowlife.

I regretted my decision. I didn't give him much energy.

He mentioned looking for work and I suggested picking up a paper. He said he couldn't read.

I started asking questions, curious how he never learned to read.

I found out that he was 3/4 Cherokee and the remainder was Navajo and Blackfoot. He was born near Memphis and his parents were killed the day he was born.

I asked how he knew and he said that somebody had helped him find a book about Indian history and read it to him. An Irish man married to an Italian woman had killed his parents and stolen him. Some kind of Indian vs. somebody feud.

Since he was 3 he's been away from his "parents." He said many people have taken him in without really wanting to know about him. He said he's always trying to find out who he is and where he came from.

He said he's lived all over. On reservations in Oklahoma and Wyoming. For some reason I didn't completely understand, the couple has wanted to kill him and have followed him. He's kind of been on the run.

I can't be certain of any of his story, of course, but I never questioned it. In the moment, being with him, it all seemed to be very possible. Or, at least, to be what he truly believed. And it seemed to fit the energy I got from him.

Recently he had been picked up by some hippies from Felton and he stayed there a while. He said for the first time he learned to settle down a little.

He said he's been accused of things he's never even considered doing. He said when he gets angry he moves on; he's gotten good at walking away from trouble.

He seemed kind of like Frankenstein. (The real Frankenstein from the novel; not the movie Frankensteins.) Solitary, unattractive, seeking his source and role, and his soul. And he seemed to harbor little real resentment in spite of his hard life.

God, it's amazing what different paths we walk.

## Flipped Out Woman on Branciforte

April 20, 1986

Santa Cruz, California

I was driving up Branciforte Drive into the mountains to meet up with my friend Heidi.

At the kid's park, a little ways out of town on Branciforte, a van was stopped half on and half off the road. As I approached, I wondered what was going on. Someone was on the ground in front of it. Car trouble? Why on the road and not pulled all the way off? There was plenty of room. It was a dirt parking area for the park. I slowed and passed and a woman jumped up from the ground, very distraught, and called to me for help. My mind was quickly entertaining various scenarios. Something violent or some conflict between her and the person or people in the van? (Who I never did get a chance to really look at.) Accident? What could it be? I pulled over, a little ahead of the van and in the parking area. She was super flipped out. Unintelligible. She came around to the open passenger window of my little VW bug. She started saying something about being followed, babies, and other mumbleations; something about esses, like the letter "s".

At first I thought she was trying to get help for someone else in trouble and in shock, then I realized it was just her. The van had bugged out, gone on its way. I never will know how that scene had developed.

She was very small and gaunt and had no trouble climbing headfirst in the window. She rolled in and curled up on the seat, upside down. She smelled bad, like drugs were in her body; that smell of the body eliminating strong medication type drugs.

She couldn't communicate anything. Unlike other flipped out people I've been around, her snatches of talk didn't say much of anything.

She had undone her pants as she had come up to my car. She eventually sat upright (more or less) in the seat. It was a warm spring day and I wasn't wearing a shirt. She reached over and felt my nipple and tried to kiss it once. I pushed her away, trying to be gentle. I felt she desperately needed affection, but I also felt that where she was at right then she wouldn't even recognize it. Just that that played some role way back in the cobwebs of her psyche, which was now tumbling out of control.

I turned the car around and headed back to town to take her to the hospital. Perhaps tranquilizers. Fight fire with fire.

So, we're heading down Branciforte. I'm trying to do my good deed for the day. All of a sudden she grabbed the steering wheel and wrenched it down with both hands, turning us to the right. At 30 mph we were heading off the road sharply. Beyond a small shoulder, it dropped off. I grabbed the wheel hard and fought against her. We swerved. I hit the brakes and we stopped.

We had just come out of the woods and were across the street from a side road and a little neighborhood. I called over to some people at a lawn party across the street. It was hard to get their attention from as far away as I was, but I did, and I had someone call the police. It took 10 or 15 minutes until they came. I sat with her, stroking her head and telling her to breathe.

Once she threw her head back and hung her tongue out, heavily coated, and I considered she might just die.

Well, the police came and I gave them a quick rundown of the story. She had curled up on the floor - and they were pretty gentle. They handcuffed her and took her off to the hospital. I supposed the handcuffs were both protocol and for her own protection in some way.

I thought the police appearing might freak her or make her feel like I had abused a trust, but it made no difference. She was beyond seeing uniforms or perceiving handcuffs.

I pray for her. Live long and prosper, woman. So strange; we souls take these bodies and abuse them, stupidly thinking we won't suffer the more for inhabiting a mistreated vehicle.

Oh my.

## Jesus Christ, On The Road

June 8, 1976
Western Washington

The day started like any other. Who would imagine that.... well....

I was in the process of moving and I had borrowed my brother Doug's old pickup truck to move my stuff down from Bellingham to Olympia. The engine seemed pretty strong but it gave off fumes and I needed to keep the windows open all the time. We'd been having the kind of weather one would expect in the spring. A little cool for June. Pretty comfortable warm sunny days, but dropping to cold crisp nights. I had worn my minimal white running type shorts going down, but had changed into some warmer clothes and was pretty bundled up driving home at night. It was a little over 3 hours drive each way. The truck was fairly loud and not a very smooth ride. I was driving the last stretch, maybe a half hour to go, of more than 6 hours of driving and was pretty frazzled.

It was about 11:30 somewhere near the Alger exit on I-5, a winding stretch through the mountains that separated Skagit Valley to the south and Bellingham to the north, when I saw a truck swerve in front of me and wondered what was up. I put myself a little bit on alert, figuring maybe an animal was in the road or debris or something. In a few seconds I found out.

A naked man (25ish, I would say) was standing in my lane, facing me, holding out his hands, waving. Did I also mention that the brakes on Doug's truck weren't that great. I screeched to a stop, just able to stop in front of him.

He came to my window and said he was Jesus Christ and Paul McCartney was Paul. He asked me if I had been listening to the radio. He referred to the first few songs of Paul's concert. I'm not usually up on the tour scene, but I think McCartney was touring in the Northwest at that time.

So, here I am, at a dead stop in the middle of a lane on the freeway, having this conversation through the open window with this naked man.

He asked me if I was a believer. It seemed very important to him. I don't remember exactly what it was I mumbled in response, but I guess he was convinced I was a believer and went around the truck and jumped in the passenger side. I drove off with him in the seat next to me.

The information I got from him wasn't exactly clear. He referring to - being hit over the eye with a pool cue - his brown eyes were turning green - Henry Kissinger was a false prophet - having been awake for several days - and earthquakes signifying God's wrath.

He told me that Bellingham was Bethlehem. And that he needed to go to the mountain and talk to God; tell Him it was ok to shake things up a little bit but not to destroy the Earth.

Mt. Baker is not far from Bellingham and to get there you take the Sunset Highway off of I-5. I guessed that is where he intended to go.

He was a pretty big man. I'm about 5'9" and 145 lbs. He was probably over 6' tall and pretty big and healthy. I wasn't really afraid, but I was a little cautious. He wasn't exactly stable. But he was also kinda nice and charismatic and more of a gentle bear than a macho guy. But, as I have experienced with people on the fringe, we weren't really communicating. He had his trip and was obsessive. At one point he turned to me, and said, "I have tremendous strength." He took hold of my right upper arm and squeezed hard. Nothing damaging, but it did hurt. I told him directly and unemotionally, "You're hurting me." He stopped right away.

He kept asking me if I believed. I continued to dance around the question, not wanting to offend or alienate him, but also not wanting to encourage him too much. We stopped for water once. He said he was very thirsty. He drank some water from a small trickle coming down the bank at the side of the road. All the time he was convinced we were going to the mountain to see his Father. He mentioned it many times and I just kinda let him believe it.

As we came into Bellingham he told me to get off at the Sunset exit, confirming my suspicions about him wanting to go to Mt. Baker.

The exit I wanted to get off at was a couple of exits before the Sunset exit. When we got to the Lakeway exit, I took it, wondering how he would react. He said, "No, no, the Sunset exit." I told him very clearly that I had been driving all day, I was really tired, and probably didn't have the gas to make it to the mountain anyway. This was my exit.

I drove down to the end of the ramp and came to a stop in front of the Sambos restaurant there. He looked at me forlornly and said, "You're not a believer." He seemed deeply disappointed that I wasn't.

He was clearly not phased by the coldness of the night, but I offered him my shorts, to protect him from the law, explaining that it might help him get around better if he wasn't completely naked. I pulled my shorts out of my backpack and gave them to him. He pulled them on. He was so much bigger than me, they were really tight; he could just barely get them on. Before he got out, he sat there a moment, contemplating. He looked at me with obvious disappointment, then looked over at Sambos, where you could see people inside, behind the big windows, eating. He said, "Look at those bing-bongs. They're not believers," opened the door of the truck and ran off towards the freeway entrance, into the Bellingham night.

Epilogue - A few days later I heard from Doug the furthering adventures of Jesus Christ. A friend of Doug's was retelling a story, that he had heard from another friend, telling him about this weird thing that happened the other night at their home. Doug instantly recognized it as the follow up to my tale.

It was the night I had dropped him off. They said that during the early morning hours of the night a man in his underwear had climbed up onto the roof of their house. Then he climbed back down and after that he got into their car. The police were called. Soon afterwards, a plainclothesman pulled up and Jesus Christ got into his car and told him to take him to the mountain. The cop said he had to wait for some friends. They showed up and he was arrested.

Wearing my shorts.

# Memorable People

### Famous Amos

October 30, 1984

It was the fall of 1984. I had gone to Connecticut to visit my friend Mary, who lived in Greenwich, Connecticut. Shortly after arriving there, I began to get sick. As it turned out, I got very sick; the sickest I'd ever been in my life. Some infection, I guess, in my upper thigh. But that's another story.

I had planned to stay a month or more, but after about two weeks or so, and no healing in sight, I knew I should return to Santa Cruz. Home and the healing Mecca that Santa Cruz is.

I called ahead to a couple of friends to see if someone could arrange to pick me up at the Oakland airport. Each of them were busy when I'd be arriving, but they assured me that they would find someone to make it up there and meet me.

Well, I arrived at Oakland really wasted. I was really sick and roadweary as well. I had traveled around a bit back East. I was pale and gaunt and I'd had a temperature for a week or so. I had pain in several places in my leg, including my knee and I had been limping for several days. So, there I was with my big backpack, barely able to walk at all and definitely not with my pack.

I arrived kind of solemnly looking forward to the mystery of who would pick me up at the airport, if in fact, someone really would. I'd had no confirmation from my friends.

Well, the mystery of who would be there to pick me up became the misery of the fact that no one was there to pick me up. I waited around a while, then finally grimly accepted the fact that I had to make it home on my own. Hitching was out of the question. Tired, defeated, in pain, I made a number of calls. To Oakland first, then through San Jose would have been a three hour bus ride. I couldn't face that. So I finally decided to take a cab to San Jose. From San Jose, there was a pretty good bus connection I could make the rest of the way.

Well, you know how taxis work. They line up and I guess you have to take them in order. They can't take someone before the cab in front, in fairness to each other. I originally went to the cab that looked the most attractive to me but was told I had to take the first one. I went to the first cab and asked him how much it would cost. It was, I think, $50 dollars to San Jose. A lot of money, but I had to get home and had to meet that bus. I agreed. He was really loose and didn't seem very professional. Normally I like a certain amount of casualness, but in my state, adventure was the last thing I wanted. I wanted comfort and security and simplicity.

He took my pack to put it into the trunk. He had to undo some bungee cords to open the trunk and then strap it closed again afterwards. I'm standing there amazed; mostly just too out of it to make any other command decisions. But when he also had to unbungee the door for me to get in, I really began to wonder what I was getting myself into. Both my door and his door needed to be bungeed closed. The inside of the car was all cut up. I was in disbelief that someone could legally run a cab in this condition.

At least he was friendly and eager. He was Black and lanky and maybe 50 years old. He told me once how old he was, but I forget exactly now. What I remember was that I was surprised how spry and young he seemed for his age. He spoke with the Black inner city kind of drawl and laughed a lot when he spoke. Again, I liked the casualness, but was concerned about the lack of professionalness.

He drove off from the airport loading area and made a stop right away, before we left the airport, to look under the hood. The car rattled in many places. Before we got on the highway he stopped at a gas station and put water and oil into a steaming radiator and smoking engine.

Finally, we got onto the freeway and were on our way. He was really friendly and talkative. This guy was loose. Just lookin' at me and talking and laughing. He asked me some questions and listened when I answered but mostly he just talked. He told me his name. "My name is Amos. Famous Amos." He obviously enjoyed his nickname.

This was so different from the time in the East. I had encountered some heavy bad vibes, and fear in people manifested in aggression, to the point of having the police called to investigate me because I had asked some kids for directions once. In fact, that energy and my inability to deal with it contributed much to my dis-ease. Famous Amos's casual nature and easy going style was exactly what I needed. My discomfort, once I accepted that the vehicle would, in fact, probably survive the trip, turned into a nice aura of security in the car. I got to really liking him.

We were too late getting to San Jose to catch the bus, so he offered to take me the rest of the way to Santa Cruz and home for $10 more; a $25 break 'cause he liked the highway cruise. So, Famous Amos would be giving me a ride all the way home for $60.

He had a friend he hadn't seen in a long time who lived in Los Gatos, a town along the way, and wanted to stop in and see him. I was a little bummed about the detour and delay but was too tired to argue. As luck would have it, his friend wasn't home and we drove on.

He dropped me right at my door, unbungeed us and my pack out of the car and I was home. Adventure was the last thing I wanted that day but I got it anyway and it turned out to be a good thing. A kind of soft personal welcome home. Thanks, Famous Amos.

## Silver Hawk Woman

December 18, 1975

I was living in Bellingham, Washington. To be precise, I was living near a lake, Lake Whatcom, four miles out of town. I didn't own a car at the time. Most days, at some point, I would go into town on the bus and meet up with friends. Then in the evening, usually after the time the buses would have stopped running, I would walk or hitchhike home. I was young and robust and sometimes I walked all the way. Other times I got lucky and got a ride or rides.

One winter night, hitching home, at the very start of Lakeway Drive, the road out to the lake, a beautiful woman in a Studebaker Silver Hawk stopped and picked me up. The Studebaker Silver Hawk is a pretty cool old car I had always liked the look of. I had seen a couple around town. She was going to Lake Louise Road, which meant she turned off about halfway to where I was going. But first she wanted to run a mile at Civic Field, a small sports complex which had a football stadium with a track around it, a little ways further down on Lakeway.

I said that sounded like a good idea and did she mind if I joined her and she thought that was a good idea. So we got there and parked the car and discovered that there was a fence and the field was locked up. I think she knew or expected that. In any case she didn't hesitate. She climbed the fence. I'm thinking, man, this woman is cool. So over I went too and out onto the track.

Keep in mind it was December and that particular night (it was about 11:30) it was freezing. It was also crystal clear out. It was really fun running. There were bleachers on both sides and because of the frozen track and cold dry air, our footfalls made a crisp sound that echoed off the bleachers. We ran six laps. It felt great. Especially to be running it with a beautiful woman under the stars, the full moon, on an icy night with a little low mist floating around.

She was very friendly, had a beautiful smile and was very vital. Alive.

So back over the fence and back in her car, she drove me to the split in the road where our paths diverged. I really didn't want the time with her to end but was too timid to suggest anything. So, we engaged in the sweetest of sorrows and parted.

# True Stories

July 6, 1977

Again, Bellingham. It was a warm summer day and thinking women, I drove off to Larabee State Park, a state park along the shores of Bellingham Bay, a few miles south of town. It didn't really fit my mood and I didn't stay long. Heading back I stopped at a place where a number of cars were parked. I had often noticed many cars parked there. I couldn't resist the urge. I'd always been curious. I'd heard rumors of some naked beaches around there, at a place called Teddy Bear Cove. So I parked and hiked the long path down to the beaches.

At one beach there was a woman sunbathing alone and reading. I struck up a conversation. She was completely open to my approaching her and we talked for quite a while. She was an interesting person. At one point she was sort of fidgeting with a small shell as we talked and kind of nervously stuck it up one of her nostrils. It kind of freaked me out. It was a small enough shell that I was a little worried that it would or could get stuck. She actually had a bit of difficulty getting it out, during which time I sensed she was maybe a little worried but she acted like she wasn't. Well, she got it out, so that was good.

At some point I decided to be bold and I asked her if she wanted to make love. No, but it was a pleasant response. She didn't seem freaked out. We continued talking for a while. That was itself encouraging, I guess.

Well, after a while, the sun was getting pretty low and we climbed up the trail together. At the top what should I see but our two cars were the only ones left. My orange VW and her Silver Hawk. Hello. Sure enough. She was the very same pretty woman who I had climbed the fence to the track and ran laps under a full moon and stars on a freezing night a year and a half ago with. Beautiful. We were both amazed. Neither of us had recognized each other. Small wonder considering the last time we were bundled up for a December night and this time we were hanging out naked in the July sun.

So it was a good day. It was encouraging to me to express myself and not have it adversely effect our conversation. She was nice company.

## Russian And Texan

July 4, 1991

Near Karlsruhe, Germany

This was the 3rd time I had gone to Europe to spend the summer. I sometimes traveled by train but often would hitchhike. While hitching, I met a Russian, who was also hitching, who was one of six who had come together, seeking sanctuary in Germany. They were given 98 Marks for a month and put in a single room. He was mildly appreciative, but that just wasn't enough for him. He was heading out with just a little satchel; not even a sleeping bag. He was small and kind of weak. He seemed really fragile but just wanted a life. Maybe Holland, maybe the U.S. He asked me lots of questions about America. I don't know exactly how he figured he'd get there but I don't think he was very clear how he'd get anywhere. He was just going. There was a kind of intensity about it. We spoke English, though his English was also weak. He was glad to talk to me, though it was not all that personal. I was just a stop along the way.

Then followed maybe the low point of my entire summer's trip. I got a ride from an absolutely dead Texan who was in the military and had been in Germany 14 years. He had been in Saudi Arabia and Kuwait for the Gulf War. He was into cars, TV's, good deals, Mom, and apple pie. A completely shallow person. He sickened me.

Interesting that these events happened on the 4th of July. What a curious juxtaposition. A gentle young Russian soul being a pioneer looking for a better life and an American embodying the worst of the arrogance and belligerence of America.

# Events And Adventures

### Pulled From The Ditch

October 8, 1991

Sonoma County, California

I had been shopping at the co-op in Cotati and when I came out my car (a Toyota station wagon) wouldn't start. That had been going on for a long time; usually starting when the engine was cold and usually not starting when it was warm. I pulled my bike out of the back and decided to take a ride over to Sonoma State University. Later, when I came back from Sonoma State the car started right up like it seems to when it's cool.

I headed off to my friend Bob's. Driving out on the country roads, I decided to get adventurous and take a road I'd seen on the map that I expected to cut through to the one I was heading for. It was dark and it was foggy and I missed it, having seen the street sign too late to slow down and turn, so I turned up the next street, a newish development looking road, to make a U turn. As I began my U turn, I saw the ditch ahead, had a glimpse of my devil may care attitude, and felt I could test it and thunk - both front wheels dropped into a deep, sharp angle-sided asphalt ditch; the car being at a 90° angle to the ditch and the road. I tried to move but no go. I got out and inspected it. It seemed that no damage was done, amazingly. It landed, well, it actually just rested on the tires but probably had bounced on the frame.

# True Stories

I knew this was really going to be a test of my grace. 10:30 at night. Cold. Foggy. Way out in the country. Looking at possible car damage and possible monumental tow truck fees.

My car was perpendicular across the narrow road. It obviously couldn't be left there overnight.

I then tried the most graceless part of the adventure. I tried to rock it out. I really taxed the clutch and motor and bounced the car on... well, I didn't really know.

I accepted the situation and figured I'd better get on the bike and head for some houselights to see if I could use a phone. There weren't many houses around but there were a couple in sight. I thought maybe I'd call my friend Nez and see if he thought his truck had the power.

So I packed up some valuables and my flashlight and opted for a house across the way, but first I stopped at the corner to use my flashlight and find out the name of the street I was on.

I was taking it all in stride actually. Kind of feeling stupid but knowing that whatever I had to pay or do, I'd pay and do and continue. Kinda grim and kinda whimsical.

I can only wonder if my several minutes of stupidly trying to rock the car out was needed for timing. Just as I was looking at the street sign a car turned into the street. I waved it down with my flashlight.

It was a young woman who lived up the hill. She was glad to help and said her Dad had a big truck. I stashed my bike back in my car and drove up with her. She introduced herself and shook hands. Her name was Tara. She was really warm and friendly.

We got to her house and she went in; I waited outside. It turns out she had to get her Dad out of bed.

Well, he got a chain and we got in his huge powerful truck.

We drove down to the car and he couldn't pull me straight because of the curb on the other side of the street. The street was too narrow. He didn't think it was going to work with the truck.

Man! Were my angels on the job or what! Perfect timing with Tara. She stops. Dad is helpful. He has a truck and chain and if that wasn't enough, a tractor!

So he went back to get the tractor. I hooked up the chain and waited. Meanwhile I tried starting the car and no go. Shit. Just what I needed.

Well, it was ages till he got back. I just stood around in the fog, wondering. Even having foolish doubts about this man, except his chain was still there.

I asked myself if I'd have faith that he would come back if I didn't still have the chain and felt disappointed in myself for doubting.

Well, he came back in the truck. The tractor wouldn't start. He was skeptical about it all and wanted to try different angles and chain connections but finally we settled on my original plan. He could back up and pull a little bit in the right direction by having the front wheels turned at a sharp angle.

Bummer that my car wouldn't start. Or would it? One more try. Hallelujah. It started. Of course. We found a place where the hook on the chain barely hung on his truck. The only place really.

He backed up. I helped a bit, using what little my car's power could contribute, and I popped right out. Nifty. We unhooked the chain and I thanked him and he went back to his well deserved bed.

I inspected underneath the front of the car and except for what the exhaust pipe may have pushed while being squished up, all seemed to be in order.

Good, helpful, warm humans. And lots of help from above.

It's even possible that if we'd tried the same plan before he went for the tractor without my car running, that it wouldn't have worked and we would have given up. Probably not, but....

Doesn't matter. Details are just how it unfolded. How it was, is that at the end of the day my car had escaped any damage, I hadn't had to spend a penny, and I was resting easy at home.

## Lake Berryessa

July 24, 1984

Lake Berryessa, Napa County, California

Late night. Oh God. What am I doing? Life is, indeed, uncertain at best.

On the positive side, I'm alive, still in relatively good health. And my possessions are in relatively good shape. And I feel relatively peaceful.

You may wonder where I am and what I've been up to. Well. I'll tell you. I am in my sleeping bag, which has only a spot soaked through, on a sloping grassy patch of ground, upon which I suspect I'll slide all night, on a tiny island in Lake Berryessa.

Now, that sounds reasonable, but there is a story behind it.

The summer before I had been up in Washington and a friend of my brother's had a rowboat for sale. It was a really slick little streamlined rowboat, not like the typical rowboat one thinks of usually, where you paddle and it practically stops before the next stroke. I guess it got its name from its performance - Screamer. It narrowed to a point at the front and to maybe two feet at the back. I was highly impressed and thought it might be fun to have a little boat, so I bought it. I built a wooden roof rack custom fit to my VW bug and took it out on a few lake adventures during the time I was up there.

Back home in California, I live in Santa Cruz. It was the middle of the summer and I thought I really ought to get out and have a little adventure. It had been quite a while since I had taken Screamer out for a row. I decided on Lake Berryessa, a lake I had driven by but had never stopped at. I had hoped to get there early and have a nice peaceful rowing and drifting time on the lake. And maybe camp on some far shore. As it turns out, I didn't get out of Santa Cruz until around 1 o'clock. I made a few stops at bookstores in San Francisco and one in Berkeley on the way. By then it was Bay Area rush hour traffic. I kept a stiff upper lip but it was, so far, not the easy cruise to the lake and a peaceful afternoon boating on the lake I had anticipated.

Well, feeling uptight, grumpy, dissatisfied, and sexually frustrated, I got to a place with a boat launch as the sun was getting very low.

I thought about it for about ten minutes, then decided to go for it. My heart had been set on it and I didn't really know what else I would do, if I didn't go for it. I put the boat in, packed it up, and headed out.

Screamer was a great little boat but, although I prefer it being wood, that can be a big problem. And that is that because it's wood, it dries out when being stored in the California dry air and sunshine and always leaks until it gets good and soaked for a while. It had been a hot day and I suspect with the heat and wind, being on the top of my car, it couldn't have been any drier.

The sun set as I was about 2/3 of the way across the lake. The boat was taking in a lot of water. I stopped rowing several times and took some time to bail it out but even so, my things were getting wet. Also with so much water in it, it had gotten much harder to row.

I finally attained the far shore, my spirits low, the sky almost dark, the boat carrying lots of water. I pulled the boat ashore and got out to reconnoiter.

The far shore was kind of a nightmare. I had hoped for some succor. Instead it seemed I was the sucker. It was midsummer and the lake was low. As I was to discover, the land was just dried up mud and rocks for quite a ways, then where it turned to field, I encountered cow pies all over. Shit! Instead of a kind of woodsy nature, I was in a rubbley cow pasture. I scouted a bit each way along the shoreline with my flashlight but didn't find anything resembling a gentle, natural place to camp. I was faced with the idea of sleeping with cows (I hadn't actually seen any but feared them showing up in the night), hiking a long ways to a place out of their field, or.....

I chose, in a real panic, to head back to a small island I had passed on the way over.

With the temperature dropping a little from the intense heat of the day, a pretty strong wind had come up. It was almost completely dark. I shoved off. Against a headwind, in choppy water.

The boat was sluggish and low in the water. Still taking on water and getting lower and slower. My rowing was kind of panicky and I was getting wet splashing the oars in the rough water.

I half expected to be abandoning all my stuff and swimming to land. I fantasized the worst. Not all that bad. The water was warm. The air was warm. It was by no means a survival situation.

Once, hiking in the Cascades with my brother in the fall we encountered a sudden weather change from mild summery weather to a heavy wind and rain storm and a substantial temperature drop. We had hiked over a ridge and a little ways down into a kind of bowl with ridges all around. There was no simple way out. We got stoned in the tent, which we had gotten set up just before dark, and just before the storm hit. When the storm first hit, before we realized how wild it would get, we thought it was cool and went outside to experience it and got soaked to the skin. When we returned to the tent we brought the wet in with us and when the storm picked up, I felt very vulnerable. I considered it might even snow; maybe quite a bit. The wind was whipping the tent around and I wasn't sure it would survive. I got kind of panicky. I mentioned trying to pack up and head out. Doug was much more levelheaded and assured me the best we could do was hang in there till morning. I accepted that. I cozied into my sleeping bag and laid on my back, wondering if I was going to die. I ran pictures of my friends across my mind and felt the love. I relaxed. I felt completely at peace and ready to accept whatever lay ahead. The storm let up.

Out in the middle of the lake, half way to the island, I imagined the boat and all of my stuff sinking to the bottom. I would swim to the island, get through an uncomfortable night, swim to shore in the morning, accept my meager losses, get in my car and get on with life. As I mellowed under the stars and began to feel downright peaceful, the wind let up, the water grew flat, and the boat seemed to stop taking in water. I had been blessed with a long twilight, being the middle of the summer, but by the time I reached the island it was totally dark. I docked by flashlight. I felt very ancient docking in this little cove at night; like a primeval act that had been carried out by humans since time immemorial.

I got everything out of the boat. I hung up all my wet clothes on the branches of a dead tree. Only my long pants and velour pullover stayed dry. And my day pack with all my non-clothes stuff. And, nicely, my sleeping bag.

So, I ate just now and it's about time to crash. It's been a hell of a day.

I think I'll check out the stars some before I go to sleep.

Good Night, My Life.

## Illegal Border Crossing

Prologue - In early June, I had come to Europe, mostly to visit and spend time with some very special friends I had made the previous summer in Tirol, Austria. In July I met a woman, Karin. We first became lovers and then without the romantic element, friends. I felt that there was a very special bond between us and that we needed time to deepen our friendship and that meant staying in Austria well into the winter. This proved worth it as she has since become my best friend but it wasn't easy. I really couldn't afford it. I had to find a place to live. It was really cold. The omnipresent smoke from cigarettes made any social life in winter impossible. I was not a happy camper. I bought a car intending to take a few escape trips south but it had serious engine issues. But I needed to get out of Innsbruck for a while. Finally, I decided to hell with caution. I decided to go and visit a friend in Switzerland, then up into S.W. Germany and visit a couple of friends there. Make a short tour of it.

My first stop was visiting my friend Robi in Luzerne. From there I was off to Germany.

So here's the story. Keep in mind that this was before the European Union and the Schengen Area and at that time crossing borders was always scrutinized.

December 15, 1986

The whole way from Luzerne to Basel, the Swiss town on the German border, the car ran poorly. The last 30 or so kilometers it was the worst it had ever been. The car was jerking so hard I thought the drive train would be ruined. It was really freaking me out. The oil pressure read really low. I had checked the oil in Luzerne and it was full, even after 350 km. of driving, which was unexpected.

So I got to the border and the German policeman asked me for the car's papers, my passport, and my driver's license. He noticed that my driver's license was invalid and had me pull over. I had no idea that my driver's license was invalid but it appeared to be so. It had expired long ago and I had never noticed. I guess the letter prompting me to deal with it had never made it to me and it just hadn't occurred to me to check it out.

He informed me I couldn't go into Germany. He handed my case over to the Swiss officials. I had to turn around and park just on the Swiss side of the border until someone could come and deal with me. I had to wait a long time, maybe a half hour, till they got back to me.

During this time I checked my oil. Still full. And discovered a tube from the motor to the carburetor was disconnected. I connected it.

The Swiss police had me follow them to a station 5 km or so down the road. The man handling my case was very friendly. When we got to this little station I was taken inside. I waited in a locked room with nothing but two desks, three wooden chairs, and a typewriter for an hour.

When he finally came back, he investigated and investigated, and eventually called the Ambassador in Vienna. He was trying to be helpful and tried to find out some information from the Embassy that would help me out. But, near as all could tell; yes, my license was invalid.

I had spent all my waiting time very solemn and resigned. The end. Not even thinking about the consequences of being in Basel unable to drive. Just feeling. Just feeling beaten down. The only thought I had was to go to Innsbruck, repair the car enough to pass the inspection (which is a whole other story) and get the sticker, repair the jerking problem, sell the car, and go home. Instead of staying until Karin was ready to accompany me back to Santa Cruz, as we had planned, I'd just have to go ahead and she'd have to fly over on her own a month and a half later.

He told me I couldn't drive in Switzerland or in Austria. Which meant, of course, I couldn't drive at all. In my emotional state I just sorta bubbled out my situation to him; not appealing to him or trying to convince him of anything. Just spilling my guts. I told him I didn't know what to do, except that he had helped me make up my mind. I told him how road weary I was, how I don't really want to live in Innsbruck, how I can't work, and about Karin. And all I wanted to do was go to Innsbruck, sell the car and go home.

He listened patiently and was very understanding. He looked at me, gave me back my papers, said, "gute Reise" ("have a good trip") and sent me off. I thanked him for his understanding.

End of phase I.

Phase II.

So, I left the place, thinking hopefully I can get the car repaired in Basel and then home, as it were, to Innsbruck. I didn't have much money either. Maybe not enough money for the repairs or for a toll at a tunnel I would have to pay to go through.

By my car, outside the little building, as I was checking out my car, I met Fredricke from Köln and an Australian man. They were heading north into Germany. We talked a few minutes. They headed off for the border but came back a couple of minutes later and asked about getting a ride to the border because there was a long tunnel ahead that didn't look like pedestrians could go through. I told them I could drive them to the border. Kinda sorta suspecting it was a stupid thing to do.

They piled in and off we went. We approached the border and I saw there was no turn around point; no exit of any kind. I was bummed. I'd have to explain what I was doing and hope they didn't think I was just trying to scam my way in and maybe get really mad. In my experience, I have encountered a lot of heaviness at borders. It's like this heavy nationalistic protective thing. Also, maybe different Swiss people would handle the situation and I'd have to start all over. The kindness from the other man would have been for nothing. Shit.

I approached the booth, this time with a different man there, slowed down, rolled down my window, prepared to blurt out apologies and appeal for understanding, and he just waved me through. He just waved me through! I was kind of freaked out. What if someone saw who had dealt with me before? I hesitated. I really didn't want any more trouble. He waved me on again, perturbed, like get on with it, man.

So I rolled into Germany. And off I went on my trip. Rolling around Europe without a driver's license, seemingly at the mercy of the Powers That Be. For better or for worse.

## The Ravine

November 2, 1986.

Austria, Tirol, The Alps

I was living in a very small village called Afling, a few kilometers west of Innsbruck. Innsbruck lies on the river Inn, which is a long deep valley cutting through the mountains with a valley floor about a mile wide. Afling was situated on a plateau a little above the valley floor. From my bedroom window I could see across the valley to the steep mountainside which was punctuated along the cliffs with deep ravines every so often that water runoff had carved.

There was one ravine directly across the valley from me that had fascinated me for the couple of months I had lived there. It was like it was calling to me. One afternoon I made a spontaneous decision to up and drive across the valley and take the plunge and hike that ravine.

Clearly, this was not planned or well thought out as I took off at about 2:30 with only a couple of hours of daylight left. It was a damp, gray day, with a little occasional drizzle.

So off I went. I drove across the valley to a place near the mouth of the ravine where I could park. And, completely unequipped, just me and my wits, such as they were, I left my car behind and dove into the woods on a sort of trail. I followed a minor ravine and came into a big gravelly open area. I tried to negotiate a difficult rocky stretch and gave it up as too dangerous. I went back down, circled around a ways and went into the woods and climbed up until I came back into the ravine not far below where there were railroad tracks skirting the hillside with a bridge that crossed the ravine. When I got to the tracks I was pretty high up. I already really felt that I had accomplished something.

Energy was absolutely free. I noted my heart and breath were both stepped up and pretty much the whole time I never rested enough to let them slow down. It was simply another gear.

Not far above the tracks I encountered a pretty difficult narrow, steep passage. I negotiated it and continued my dialogue with my angels. And with myself. Asking for strength to continue, but sense to know my limits.

Shortly after, I came to a place where a big boulder was wedged into a narrow place and jutting out. I tried several times to negotiate it, then considered a circle along the wall. At this point in the ravine there was little relief from the steep walls, so I gave that idea up. I piled up a few stones and that gave me the extra foot I needed to get enough friction on the top and haul myself over.

A while later I encountered another slightly difficult area. It wasn't too hard, but I began to question if there had been more than the two especially difficult places and how hard they might be to negotiate, going the other direction. I had it in my mind to get to the woods at the top, circle a little, and cruise down through the woods. Later, back in the valley, upon viewing the mountain, I was forced to face the fact that my power of observation or memory or both leave a lot to be desired. The whole mountain is sheer cliffs and a few ravines, mostly more rugged than the one I was in. But even without that knowledge, I considered I might need to come back down the same way.

Then came a long stretch of basically walk-climbing, occasionally scrambling.

Time was passing and I had to make decisions. Every bend and horizon was an illusion, offering false hopes of reaching something leveler and tamer. I came to a place where it got very narrow and climbed a lot. Here there was a sloping wall on the left side. I considered leaving the ravine proper and climbing along that slope a ways. I decided to try it and climbed out of the middle of the ravine. I went up a ways, soon discovering a cave. It was leeward and totally protected and dry. If I had to I could survive a night there.

I found that the slope offered no exit, but also discovered I could go over a hump and come into the ravine further up, avoiding the narrow steep section, much of which I couldn't see.

From the high point on the hump I could see the ravine opening into woods. I was excited, thinking I had achieved my goal. Silly me. It was pretty straight forward and I headed up, choosing the most rational of the four or five smaller ravines it branched out into.

But quickly I saw it was futile. About this time the running dialogue in my head was getting a little nervous. I realized up was foolish. I wondered what else might be foolish. I again tried to bail out of the ravine. No go. I knew heading down the ravine was the only reasonable way, maybe the only possible way, and maybe the only way I would survive. The grayness was even, and time was hard to judge but I reckoned an hour was the most daylight I could possibly have. It had become a little windy and shortly it would rain a few moments, throwing slip-concern into the picture. I sensed sunset weather change possibilities.

Here I took time for the first time and only time in the climb. I waited till my heart and breathing were almost normal. That required some time, because the previous 5 or 10 minutes had been especially strenuous with semi-panicky explorations.

I was really high up. The cloud level across the valley was too low to offer much view, but I was up there. Well up above the village of Götzens and any of the plateaus on the other side of the valley.

So, with questions due to a faulty memory, I headed down. Knowing it would be faster, colder, (up to this point I was totally warm) and very possibly, more dangerous.

I was a little impatient, and tried to balance this with common sense. I slipped and slid at a good pace for a while and came to the stretch I had gone around. It had begun to rain lightly and a bit of wind had come up. But.... it would be much faster to go through the ravine instead of back along the slope, so I tried it.

Immediately came a place where I knew it would be difficult to climb back up should I have to. Still, I jumped it down and threw caution to the wind, though I felt the craziness. I felt panicky. Pretty intense. Around a curve and instantly another jump. This one would be very hard to climb back up. 2 ½ - 3 feet apart walls and virtually no holds. There just couldn't be still another obstacle in this short stretch I had circumnavigated. I jumped - insane. 10 more yards and.... a no holds, narrow, 15 foot jump. The moment of truth. I was freaking. Part of me said, don't panic. Another part said, "go ahead and panic. It's good for you." I did. Without looking to the side, back, or at any time down, I ran back to the narrow place I had just jumped down and threw myself into a wedging, friction oriented sort of climb against the 2 walls. Twice I belted out the strongest sounds I've ever heard coming from my gut as I let a hold go and thrust upwards, one lunge after the other. I pulled it off. One down and one to go. I ran up to the next (not as serious as the first) and similarly scrambled and frictioned against the wall my way up. I pulled it off.

That was total animal. That was action. I don't know if I've ever thrown myself into anything like that before. Trapped, I guess. The jump down at the last obstacle may have been survivable, but these rocks were hard.

So, still a little nervous, I scooted up over the hump and using trees, negotiated the slope and the detour without problems.

From here on it was a long stretch to the two or, I wondered, more difficult passages. Every little ways I would look out at the valley. It seemed that every time I looked out I'd marvel at how much I'd come down and every time I'd have to face the reality that I was still way up this mountain.

Finally I got to the two (it was just two) tricky places. They required a little caution and short jumps but no real problem.

I saw the train bridge and felt like I was home.

I cut into the woods and discovered again how high I really was. Back into the ravine I skied loose rocks a little ways and that was divine.

I encountered a few more obstacles and circled back into the woods. It was getting dark and I took my worst fall of all in the woods. Not bad, but a reminder.

So I made it. I came out 30 feet from the car. Civilization and ease.

One curious note. I experienced a lot in 2 ½ hours; many, many individual events. But the one thing that sticks in my head and leaves me with the feeling of the worst nightmare is a brief moment during the long free stretch coming down.

There was a cliff on one side - not smooth but no real holds. And on the other side was a huge, amazingly smooth for nature slab. They came together in a wedge. I slid down, one foot ahead of the other. At one point, somewhat similar to what I've experienced in trees, my foot began to wedge in, driven by my weight. I almost ignored it, but then I got a picture of my weight driving my foot in, my back to the rocks and no hand holds or foot holds to pull or push my weight back up. The situation passed as quickly as it had arisen. But, still, I freak now when I think of those innocent little things.

And what might have been.

The Truth Seeker's Handbook

# Messages From The Universe

### Loneliness is Such a Drag

August 2, 1994
Maui, Hawaii

From my home in Makawao I had hitch-hiked in to Kahului to do some errands. I was a bit frazzled and just wanted to get home.

At the edge of town where I began my hitch back, I put it out that I wanted a comfortable ride, meaning physically. Nice car. Out of the wind. Not the back of a pickup. Then I thought a little and added that I wanted a soft warm vibe with the driver too.

As it turns out the first ride I got was from three drinking, smoking, ugly awful men in the little back seat of a jeep.

So, I'm thinkin', like, man, where is my power of imagining?!!! The next ride was good vibes but also windy in a jeep.

I thought, well maybe I just failed to exercise my power of choice and turn down those rides.

I walked along the beach a ways to the next town, Paia, where I needed to turn inland for the last stretch homeward. I went to the hitching spot at the edge of town for one last ride 7 miles uphill to Makawao.

Shortly someone stopped, offering me a ride in a groaty, filthy pickup truck back. I turned it down. So far so good. Using my power of choice to turn down something undesirable. I had been immediately given the opportunity to put to use the idea that had come to me.

Then two cars stopped right by me and the drivers got out and one was as intense as I've ever seen a man, very dangerous, and wanting to pulverize the other. He had seen the other man and had waved him down to stop. This man reeked of danger. I felt no compulsion to intervene to help my brother. From what they were saying, the aggressor, a big, strong, macho guy, felt they had unfinished business and he was going to finish it by smashing the guy. The other guy backed away slowly while the big guy pressed him, and they backed away down the street this way. Eventually they mellowed some as the littler guy's pleas for mercy were heard.

All this while music was coming out of the aggressor's still open car door. Reggae singing Jah Love. Uh-huh.

They had stopped their cars right uphill from me and started their confrontation right next to me. I had bailed and gone to the other side of the street. When they had moved down a ways, I had crossed back over to resume hitching.

A car stopped and I took the ride; just wanting away from there. A cigarette smoking, drinking, completely unattractive man in a shitty truck about to disintegrate. Friendly though.

What a weird day! I sure wish I knew what I was supposed to have learned from that sequence of events.

Epilogue - Two weeks later, hitching back from Kahului, I got picked up by the guy who was wanting to pulverize the other guy. In his big jacked up flashy jeep. He had a bandaged and/or braced right hand. This time, Burning of the

Midnight Lamp was playing. Hendrix singing, "loneliness… is such a… drag." It seemed ironic. The juxtaposition of Hendrix's sensitivity to the macho hoax. Yes. Loneliness is such a drag, my friend.

## Woman Yells, "I want sex!" At Me

Jan. 25, 1982
Santa Cruz, California

I had been out doing some errands on my bike and I was riding home. Just a few blocks from home I rode by a house where there was a woman standing, talking to some friends in a car in the driveway and I heard her say, "I haven't been laid in so long" pretty loud and with feeling. She noticed me and we made eye contact and knowing that I must have heard what she had just said, she yelled out even louder to me and the world, "I want sex!" I looked and smiled and rode on thinking about it. Had she been alone I would have gone right back but I thought it would be pretty awkward trying to communicate my feelings with her friends there. But I decided to anyway. I rode back and stopped on the road close by but she had her head in the car and didn't see me. I waited for a few seconds, then felt weird and rode a block away and stopped and thought about it for 15 minutes. I saw her friends leave and I went back but she was no longer outside in the driveway.

It was a little reassuring, in a way, to know that there was a woman out there who was feeling the need as I was. She expressed it with such passion and frustration. It made me realize that I shouldn't always feel that I'm asking a favor, wanting sex, but that I have something to give. I always believe that, but my insecurity belies it all too often. It got me to thinking about sex as sex and why not, and sex as communication and sharing with a friend.

## Too Many Coincidences

As a subset of Messages From The Universe these are a few stories which are not big event stories, but I find them worthy of note; they seem to fit into the category of events in my life that I refer to as "too many coincidences". It's like there is a point when it seems like it is not just a coincidence, but a message from the universe to be paid attention to.

## Rogers in Idaho

August 25 & 26, 1977

I was spending the summer in the Sawtooth Mountains in Idaho working with my roommate / work partner building a cabin for his parents. We lived at the site. It was just a hundred yards or so from where we were working under the trees to a big open meadow, Goat Meadows, with fantastic views. When I had time and often at the end of the workday I would go there and read or just look out. One day after work I was kind of drifting around, just taking it in and encountered another man doing the same. We stopped and talked a while, enjoying each other. Finally, we got around to introducing ourselves. I said, "My name is Roger." He smiled and said, "My name is Roger." That's always fun; Roger isn't extremely rare but I don't meet all that many. We asked each other our last names. His was Browning. We were both amazed. Not just the names but how we'd met and it was kind of like a little reflection. Roger Brown and Roger Browning.

Well, the next day, as I was heading again out to Goat Meadows to mellow out, I met a couple at a trail head, which was right where the road ends and opens up into the meadow. They were just getting out of their car and preparing to go for a hike. He and I started talking. We enjoyed each other and got into it a little. She went ahead up the trail. Finally we prepared to part and introduced ourselves. "My name is Roger." "My name is Roger." Too much. Far out. I told him of my meeting the day before. Again, we asked each other our last names. His was Roger Brink. Not quite as close as the day before, but it still seemed amazing. Another Roger Br..... Wild.

With both of these meetings what struck me as most interesting, beyond the coincidence, was that in both cases we shared such a nice easy rapport and I felt right from the moment I encountered each one that they were very appealing gentle souls.

## A Strange Phone Call

September 7, 1984

I had just laid down to sleep, feeling really tired. A really clean it's been a full day and it's the right time to sleep tired. Not that half wired tired from staying up past the best time.

I was slipping away on my back, which is nice and a rare thing for me. I was focusing on the space between my thoughts. And it was really feeling good.

The phone rang bringing me back to wakefulness and I answered it. Some woman, whose voice reminded me of the mother of a couple of friends of mine, a kind of nagging voice, asked me if I was Roger Brown. I said I was. Then she asked if I knew where my grandparents were. I said, "yeah, dead." She proceeded to go into a tirade about me, asking why I didn't tell my brother Wayne. (I have no brother Wayne) I hardly had a chance to get a word in as she went on about how inconsiderate I was and what kind of son and brother I was. She was extremely vindictive. I just kind of laid there and took it in, shocked out of the mellow state I had been in. I also found it curious that my answer that my grandparents were dead seemed to fit right in with whatever the facts were regarding who she thought I was.

I told her finally that she certainly had the wrong person. She wouldn't listen at first. It took a while to get through to her. I asked how she got my number. She had gotten it from information. It never was completely clear to me if there was supposed to be another Roger Brown in Santa Cruz who she was trying to reach or what the family drama was that she was referring to.

Upon discovering and finally believing she had gotten the wrong person, she paused, then apologized several times. She told me she was an angry woman and deeply sorry for the mistake.

Also it must have been very spontaneous on her part, because it was pretty late at night. And me being on the west coast, if she was anywhere east, it would have been even later.

I wondered if, in the state I was in, how I was really opening to the spaces between thoughts, I had loosened the fabric of space and it was somehow a product of that.

## Roger Brown, the Famous Author

February 5, 1985

Northern California

Two days earlier in Santa Cruz, I had met a woman, Sari, at the big Sunday Flea Market. We talked for a long time. We discovered we both knew of and liked Harbin Hot Springs, a nice hot springs community in Lake County, northeast of Napa. We made plans to go up there together a couple of days later.

Sari and I took separate cars because she wanted to go up sooner than I did and we each wanted to visit a couple of different people along the way. But we planned to meet in Petaluma at a friend of her's house to spend the night before we went on to Harbin.

When I got to her friend Rainbow's house, Sari introduced me to her as "Roger." Rainbow got this interested look on her face and asked me, "Roger Brown?" "Yes." Then, "Roger Brown from Seattle?" "I live in Santa Cruz now but I grew up in Seattle and lived in the Northwest mostly for 30 years." "Do you write; are you an author?" "Well, not exactly an author, but I have been writing journals for 10 years." "Have you published anything?" "No." "Well, you will."

She went on to explain that she had had a dream several months ago where she met a Roger Brown from Seattle who was a famous author. She was excited meeting me because since the time that she had the dream she has wondered when I would appear and she would meet me in real life.

Epilogue - The next day we all went to Harbin. There was lots of construction going on and I decided not to stay. I hadn't really felt much personal affinity with Sari or Rainbow and didn't stay in touch with them. I don't think I've seen either of them since. But her dream image had enough details that fit, so I've always wondered. It's now 30 years later. I'm finally putting my writings together, with the hopes of offering them to the world. As of this moment, I am not famous. At least not on this plane. I guess time will tell.

## Wrong Number

July 2, 1995
Kauai, Hawaii

It was a curious day. I had three little seemingly cosmic occurrences.

First, I saw a some sort of white sphere in a pool at Secrets Beach and reached down and pulled it out. It was a golf ball. On it, it said "4 Pinnacle Gold". It seemed to be telling me to go for the highest.

Next, I found at Ha'ena Beach a shell left on a bench that is in an incredible figure 8 shape. It also looked like the ampersand symbol and then later I noticed it looked a little like chambers of the heart. Quite an incredible shell.

Thirdly, I called into my answering service and a woman named Renee Rock from Michigan was asking if I knew how to get a hold of a couple who were supposed to be giving tours of the island's spiritual or cosmic qualities and places. She thought I might know as a member of the "metaphysical community."

I called her back and we talked a bit. I told her spirituality was integral in my life, but I was part of no such "community" and knew of no such people or tours. I asked how she got my name or number and she said she found a flyer or something posted with my number that said something like, "I feel duty bound to offer spiritual guidance. Please call."

Amazing. Wrong number and total coincidence?

Or divine intervention giving me a nudge, helping me give of myself that which I can't seem to initiate on my own?

## At The Cliffs

April 10, 1988

Santa Cruz, California

I was feeling really disappointed in life. Things just didn't seem to be working out. I had the feeling that someday I would be released and I would be free, but right then my sentence seemed too long and too harsh. (We are our own judge, jury, sentencer, and executioner.) It just seemed like the only sense I could see in all of it was that I was supposed to learn to be gracious in defeat.

I decided to get on my bike and take a ride along the cliffs by the ocean and see if that would help. I bought a bottle of beer along the way to drink somewhere, sitting looking out over the ocean. That's a rarity for me. Not the sitting looking out over the ocean part. The drinking a beer part. I hardly ever drink anything alcoholic. It seemed fitting that when I got settled, ready to drink it, the top wouldn't even unscrew. It took me 10 minutes just to open my beer. I rummaged around in my pack and the only thing I found that remotely resembled an appropriate tool was my bike tire gauge and I cut myself in several places doing it. It seemed like a curious metaphor. The gauge measures pressure.

## True Stories

After that I rode to the bench at the foot of 24th Avenue, where I often go to sit and enjoy the beach and the ocean. The bench was already occupied. A young man was spilling out his life story to an older man, saying how he tries to learn from mistakes and find a way to always improve but nothing works no matter how hard he tries. I stood, leaning on my bike, listening in for a while. He was so intent and unashamed, he was not disturbed by the fact that I was easily within earshot. He was spilling out his guts; it was my story. One disappointment after another. He was really sincere and really couldn't figure it; how it just never came together. The older man mostly sat patiently and listened; took it in; just being there for him.

When I got back home, for some reason, I up and turned on the TV and stumbled onto a show that featured a piece about a man, named Roger, who was paralyzed and confined to a wheelchair. TV Roger told about how he learned to appreciate life. He's studying to be a teacher. And he told about a wonderful, loving, intimate physical relationship that has come into his life. And there was footage of both of them and a bit about her story too. Her appreciation of him.

In my family, my father was paralyzed from the waist down and had been in a wheelchair since I was 5 years old. Of the four members of our family, myself, my brother, my Mom, and my Dad, he was, while alive, without question the happiest and most at peace with himself.

It sure seemed like somebody out there scripted that day for me.

# About the Author

I was born in Seattle and spent the first 30 years of my life in the Pacific Northwest. Well, except for 4 school years in a private Quaker boarding school in Pennsylvania, which was a great communal living experience. I think this had a far reaching and profound effect on my life. I have since lived in many different places, mostly favoring the West Coast; Olympia, Bellingham, San Juan Island, San Luis Obispo, Santa Cruz, Santa Fe, Maui, Kauai and currently Sebastopol, California. Integral in my experience has been a number of trips to Europe, mostly spending my time in the area around Innsbruck, Austria, which is my second home and where I have so many dear friends.

Work has also been varied; most of it being for myself. I have worked as a carpenter and with a partner built 2 houses in the mountains (one in Idaho, one in Washington) using (almost) exclusively hand tools. In Santa Cruz, I started my own business building and selling portable massage tables of my own design and did that for many years.

I love music; my favorites being classical music of the more sublime nature (Debussy, for one) and psychedelic era rock of which I consider the Beatles to be the ultimate. My favorite instrument is the human voice. Music has been a cornerstone of my life and has carried me through many peaceful and turbulent times.

I love to get out and ramble around on my mountain bike. It keeps me young; not the exercise so much as the playfulness and freedom of it.

And my most recent passion is playing strategic eurogame board games with friends.

# Other Books by Roger Brown

**The Truth Seeker's Handbook** has been published in print and as an eBook. I kept journals for over 20 years, writing almost every day. Much of the philosophy, the struggles leading to learning and the attitudes that helped me get through life appears in this book. It has a section dealing with major life themes, one about our relationship to the Earth, one retelling stories of serendipity, and finally a section of reminders to help along the way.

Two of those sections are available as their own books:

> Themes of my Life
> Reminders From Life for Life

Excerpt from The Truth Seeker's Handbook:

> Delight in truth at all costs. We really must accept everything we experience. Simply say, yes, this is happening to me. We tend to avoid and repress and choose against less pleasant feelings. What a rip-off! They offer powerful information as to what is going on; information as to the reason why we don't at the moment have pleasant feelings. The desirable feelings validate flow and rightness. The unpleasant ones are the ones needing the most attention.

- - -

**Insights** has been published in print and as an eBook. This is a compilation of most of the journal entries which didn't appear in any of my other books, but that I felt needed to see the light of day. I organized them into such categories as Cosmic, Philosophy and Attitude, Love, Society, and several more.

Excerpt from Insights:

I heard Earth Angel on the radio today and thought about the American Dream and its surfacing in the 50's and the dreamy songs reflecting it. I was overwhelmed with a rush of rightness. Sure it is distorted. Sure its means are destructive. But the dream - to have comfort and ease and the time and space to relax and expand, time to create, to have comfortable homes is fine. It sparked a spiritual movement which unfortunately was complicated by an awesome opportunity to be corrupted by material and sensory numbing diversions. But the dream itself, it's not only the American Dream but a soul's dream. To mellow a life in a body. To find harmony. I'm all for it.

- - -

**Heading Out** is poetry and prose and has been published in print and as an eBook. Cryptic and cosmic might be good words to describe these writings; word adventures. Poetry is an individual thing and I can't say for sure you will like them, but look for it and check out the free eBook sample.

A short poem from Heading Out:

> Popsicle process brings freedom ... in heat.
> What was ice yields a watery treat.
> When we allow ourselves to have what we need
> That water fertilizes and brings life to our seed.

- - -

**Encounters** has been published in print and as an eBook. It is about encounters with women in my life that were romantic and sometimes intimate but does not include the girlfriends or lovers of duration. It is all journal entries in real time; usually my initial feelings, the encounter evolving, and finally myself seeking resolution and completion for myself and hopefully us. These encounters took place mostly during my 20's and 30's and are very gutsy and emotional. I have been a very emotional person and it may surprise some people to read a man's feelings essentially unedited.

Excerpt from Encounters:

> I approached her during a thunderstorm downpour on the main sunning deck (at Harbin Hot Springs). I was attracted to her and felt an immediate thrill from and affection for her. I wanted her. I spent some time with her and got to know her a little. I slept next to her on the sleeping deck. She let me know she needed space. She removed my hand gently from her body, but didn't let go. She held my hand a few moments more. What a beautiful softening of the space between us that she required. I was hurt and felt rejected, although I appreciated her communication and integrity. I cried. Strange sleep. Dreams. I felt again defeated but fought it, hung in there.

- - -

**33 Years of Dreams** has been published in print and as an eBook. Over a period of 33 years I wrote down a ton of dreams. A friend once said to me, why would anybody want to read anyone else's dreams? That got me to thinking but it came to me you could also ask why would anybody want to read anyone else's poetry? They are the same, in a way; kind of cryptic non-linear stories that take images and create something to be interpreted. After trimming out some of the uninteresting and poorly transcribed dreams it is, in its final form, almost 700 pages and is published in 2 volumes. They are for sale individually.

A dream from 33 Years of Dreams:

> I was with a pet, female, smiling Buffalo and a group of friends hanging out in the country. And with an alien friend who materialized to be with us. There was a river scene, after going through a gate. Rednecks were hassling us, then we saw three of our women being physically abused down the road a ways, by three men. We headed down in force (with our alien and Buffalo) to deal with it.

## Where to Buy the Books

To buy the books in print go to my Author Page: http://books2read.com/rogergoldenbrown

Versions of these books in eBook format can all be found at Smashwords, as well as free sample downloads: https://www.smashwords.com/profile/view/Rogue17

Check out my Smashwords author interview here: https://www.smashwords.com/profile/view/Rogue17154

## Appreciation

A warm thank you and appreciation for all the friends that were there for me along the way. Especially Karin, Russ, Fred, Keith, my brother, mother, and father, George School, Santa Cruz, and all the water I have swum in.

Please contact me should you want to comment or ask about anything. Also I would appreciate any feedback if any typos are discovered.

wordsmith@goldengalaxies.net

Thanks for reading.

www.ingramcontent.com/pod-product-compliance
Lightning Source LLC
LaVergne TN
LVHW041613070426
835507LV00008B/212